ANDREW MURRAY
WONDERBOY

ANDREW MURRAY
WONDERBOY

EUAN REEDIE

JOHN BLAKE

Published by John Blake Publishing Ltd,
3 Bramber Court, 2 Bramber Road,
London W14 9PB, England

www.blake.co.uk

First published in paperback in 2006

ISBN 1 84454 265 3

British Library Cataloguing-in-Publication Data:

A catalogue record for this book is available from the
British Library.

Design by www.envydesign.co.uk

Printed in Great Britain by William Clowes Ltd, Beccles, Suffolk

1 3 5 7 9 10 8 6 4 2

Papers used by John Blake Publishing are natural, recyclable products made
from wood grown in sustainable forests. The manufacturing processes
conform to the environmental regulations of the country of origin.

ACKNOWLEDGEMENTS

The author would like to thank Andrew Murray for providing such interesting subject matter, the author's parents for their unstinting love and support, Ruth Nickson for her helpful comments and Nick Callow for allowing him to work on this biography.

EUAN REEDIE has been a sports journalist and football reporter for three years, writing for a variety of leading publications, newspapers and magazines worldwide. Born in Dunfermline, Scotland, in September 1976, Euan studied English Literature and French at St Andrews University. He has lived in Plymouth since 1988. Author of the bestselling *Alan Shearer: Captain Fantastic*, this is his second biography.

CONTENTS

INTRODUCTION

MEET ANDREW MURRAY, a young Scottish tennis sensation whose astounding emergence from provincial Scotland and relative anonymity to world wide renown is truly the stuff of comic books and fairy tales.

In less than a year, this extraordinary teenager has turned professional and galloped up the tennis rankings with bewildering haste, enormous courage and marvellous skill. He captured the hearts and minds of a success-starved British tennis public by excelling at Queen's Club and at Wimbledon, as well as revitalising his country's moribund Davis Cup team with his swagger and passion, vigour and verve.

Not content with leaving a lasting impression on his homeland, amazing Andy Murray then set about winning global acclaim by triumphing in America and then reaching the final of the Thailand Open.

But while this Scottish tyro's trip to the top has been awe-inspiring and success-filled, it has also been troubled and tragic. He cowered in his headmaster's office while tragedy unfolded at his primary school during the 1996 Dunblane massacre, and his rapid teenage growth has induced both painful cramps and anguished expressions in some of the most celebrated tennis theatres in the world.

In 2004, Andy Murray reaches the third round of the junior tournament at Wimbledon.

Yet these brushes with adversity and the boy's bouncebackability are central to the shaping of the Murray phenomenon. 2005 and early 2006 would be for Murray the best of times and the worst of times. For the rest of use they would herald a new era of excellence and excitement in British tennis.

Now, sit back and wonder at the Wonderboy...

Chasing the American dream: Murray defeats German Mihail Zverev 6-3-6-2 to reach the final of the boys' singles at Flushing Meadows in the US Open of 2004.

CHAPTER I

MURRAY MANIA

THE YEAR 2005 was, for Andrew Murray, unarguably the greatest in his teenage life. In just 12 short months he romped up the tennis rankings, from outside the Top 400 to the dizzy heights of 64th. Along the way he put in some unforgettable performances in some of the world's greatest arenas.

Displaying verve and gusto in abundance, masses of guts and determination and a voracious lust for victory, he remarkably reached the second round in nine out of ten tournaments to become the first teenager from the UK to rank in the world's Top 100 since Buster Mottram in 1974. In so doing, he leapt from relative anonymity to firstly achieve household renown and then celebrity status, outstripping Tim Henman as Britain's tennis darling and reviving domestic interest in a game,

Andy Murray with his girlfriend Kim Sears.

which, outside the Wimbledon fortnight, is barely regarded by most people in Britain.

In particular, Murray's youthful exuberance, passion and pugnacity endeared him to an eager young audience in a way that the aloof housewife's choice Tim Henman, or the plucky-but-limited Greg Rusedski, could only dream of. And as his pile of notable scalps mounted, from Radek Stepanek to

3

Taylor Dent and Robby Ginepri, so the world began to take notice, too. Combative defeats against established heavyweights such as David Nalbandian and the peerless Roger Federer only added to the Scottish tyro's growing reputation. Before long a host of celebrity devotees, from footballers to film stars, boxers to politicians, were queuing up to salute the rising young star.

But if 2005 was Murray's breakthrough year, it inevitably begged the question: what next? Even as the 'A Star is Born' headlines were being written by some commentators, others were asking if Murray would be able to withstand the pressure of having too much too soon. Was he a flash in the pan, the experts asked, or was Tim Henman's long reign as Britain's number one over for good? More importantly, would he do something about his straggly, unmanageable hair? The fact that the style pundits were taking an interest in this new kid on the block was a sure sign that he'd arrived!

'ANDY IS GOING TO BE ONE OF THE TOP GUYS IN THE WORLD. HE'S GOING TO BE A TOP 10 PLAYER.'

John McEnroe

While opinion is still divided on what to do with Murray's tumbling locks, less controversial is the

Old masters
such as John
McEnroe soon
rated Murray
as a rising star.

degree of consensus among tennis fans and experts alike that this boy is the real deal. Writing in *Scotland on Sunday*, journalist Moira Gordon pointed out that: 'Following a series of displays which have signalled his true potential, the 18-year-old now has a list of famous names willing to testify in his favour.' In December 2005 the ever-opinionated John McEnroe, commenting in *The Scotsman*, nailed his colours firmly to the mast, claiming that: 'Andy is going to be one of the top guys in the world. He's going to be a top ten player, most likely. He'll probably be in the Top 20 by Wimbledon.'

Never one to willingly be outdone by McEnroe, Jimmy Connors added his name to the roll call of Murray supporters that same year. Enjoying a stint as a BBC commentator during Wimbledon 2005 Connors, famed for his combustible temper and raging will to win, was won over by Murray's rich reservoir of talent and never-say-die commitment to the cause. After coolly analysing the Scottish prodigy's strengths and weaknesses, Connors delivered the following verdict: 'Andy's game is there. He's got all the shots, he has power, he has finesse, he has a very good first serve. His whole game as an 18-year-old is very mature.' Asked what Murray needed to do

> **'Andy's game is there. He's got all the shots,'**
> Jimmy Connors

to take him on to the next level, Connors advised: 'Maybe a little bit more work on the court to improve his conditioning and strength. Once he can incorporate that into this game, then he will be spectacular.'

Later in the year, Connors would further demonstrate his appreciation of Murray's abilities by personally approaching the Scot and asking him to participate in a proposed DVD offering tennis instruction. His co-stars would be Chris Evert, Boris Becker and world number one doubles team Bob and Mike Bryan. It was quite an honour for an 18-year-old and a sure sign that Jimmy Connors, for one, knew that Andrew Murray had what it takes to succeed.

'I THINK MURRAY IS THE NEXT BRITISH STAR. I CAN'T REALLY SEE ANY WEAKNESSES IN HIS GAME,'

Björn Borg

The next tennis legend to join the Murray fan club was Björn Borg, five-times Wimbledon winner and holder of 11 Grand Slam titles. A man of few words. Borg's assessment of Murray is terse but emphatic: 'I think Murray is the next British star. I can't really see any weaknesses in his game. He is an extremely talented player.' Ice cool on the court, Borg knew a thing or two about keeping his emotions in check and offered the following advice: 'One thing I think he is going to have to work on is his temper. He needs to control his emotions on court. However, he is only young, only a teenager, and he is going to learn so much. I think he has a great future.'

No line-up of the world's tennis greats would be complete without nine-times Wimbledon women's champion, Martina Navratilova. Sure enough, she was as enthralled as her male counterparts by British tennis's brightest new talent. 'He has one of the most complete games in men's tennis,' she says. 'Andy can obviously adapt and tailor his game around who he's playing next. He's got the slice backhand, the heavy ground strokes, and he can serve and volley.'

> 'I think Murray is great. It's going to be exciting watching him develop as a player. I think he's one of Britain's best young sportsmen.'
>
> David Beckham

Murray was understandably flattered by the high praise he was receiving from the tennis world's high priests. 'Having these people saying such nice things is unbelievable because of the amount of respect I have for them,' he remarked. 'Some of the greatest players ever are telling me that I can be at the top and it gives me a lot of belief. And it sort of makes people realise that maybe it is not just hype.'

One sportsman who knows more about hype than most is David Beckham. Inevitably, as with most things, the England captain was asked to give his verdict on Scotland's new superstar after watching him in action at the Madrid Masters tennis tournament in 2005. 'It's good to have new people coming through in tennis,' he said. 'We've obviously got Tim Henman and Greg Rusedski already, but it's great for our country that we've got a talented young player like Murray coming through. I think Murray is great. It's going to be exciting watching him develop as a player. I think he's one of Britain's best young sportsmen.'

Murray was perhaps so taken aback by this glowing testimonial from British sport's biggest star that, in response, he revealed that he would support the England football team at the 2006 World Cup. What his fellow Scots though of this is, perhaps, fortunately unrecorded. However, it does demonstrate that Murray is very much a *British* tennis player, someone who is out there giving his all for the entire nation.

As the accolades came pouring in for Murray, his coach Mark Petchey unwittingly sparked a good-natured controversy when he claimed that if

Murray's progress continued at the same level he would soon be more popular than the England and Manchester United soccer star, Wayne Rooney.

Journalists on both sides of the border eagerly joined the debate. Writing in *The Scotsman* Eve Fodens pointed out that: 'While it is true that Murray is taller than the England football sensation is ever likely to be, it would take a fair stretch of the imagination to consider a tennis player becoming "bigger" than a footballer in a country such as Britain, where the population's tennis obsession lasts for only two weeks before it is engulfed by an unstoppable infatuation with soccer.'

The Sunday Times's Hugh McIlvaney issued a stern rebuke to Petchey for his admittedly only half-serious comments. 'Mark Petchey, did [Murray] no favours by declaring he could be bigger than Wayne Rooney, who just happens to be one of the very best players now active in the planet's most popular sport,' he wrote, adding: 'We have every right to celebrate Andy Murray but let's wait until he has at least a few minor titles in the bag before deafening ourselves with nationalistic trumpet-blowing.'

Leaping to Murray's defence, Sue Mott of *The Daily Telegraph* believed that the short-tempered Rooney would do well to learn from Murray's example. She rightly pointed out that:

Murray gets the British grass-court season off to a good start at the Stella Artois tournament at Queen's Club, London, in June 2005.

The theory is that Rooney will grow up. He is only 19. He is only a teenager and you know what Kevins they can be. In fact, 19 is not that young. You can vote, drink, drive, marry and join the Army. Some sort of rational thought is allowed to penetrate the cranium at that stage. You can be considered a responsible person. Proof lies in another sporting teenager, Andy Murray, a year younger than Rooney. He clearly has a fiery temperament, too, being of proud Scottish descent and a waspish nature in his pursuit of global tennis domination. Like Rooney, he has played some big matches. None bigger than last Sunday when he faced Federer in the final of the Thailand Open. At this level, tennis is a pugilistic sport. One-on-one, all flaws open to the most severe examination. No hiding place. Murray could have been humiliated. Instead, he carried himself bravely to a no-disgrace result and the resounding praise of those who watched him, including Federer himself. The young Scot lost 6-3, 7-5 to the greatest tennis talent on earth and berated himself furiously. But not the umpire, not the crowd and not the opposition.

'YOU CAN ALWAYS LEARN A LOT FROM WATCHING OTHER PLAYERS. I AM NEVER SATISFIED WITH MY OWN PERFORMANCE. THERE ARE ALWAYS AREAS WHERE I CAN IMPROVE.'

Sue Mott was not the first person to comment on Andrew Murray's short fuse. His intermittent explosions of rage on court offered a stark contrast to British tennis's other big star, Tim Henman, whose 'Tiger Tim' nickname belied a placid, almost introverted on-court persona. But Murray's outbursts came purely from a desire to win – and frustration at his inability to do so against opponents such as Roger Federer. In time, the experts agree, Murray will learn to channel his anger in more positive directions. In this respect, they point to Roger Federer himself – now a paragon of calm self-assurance, the Swiss star was once prone to youthful displays of foot-stomping angst similar to those experienced by Murray. Once he had learned to control his demons, and convert his anger into positive energy, Federer simply became unbeatable. If Andrew Murray demonstrates an ability and a willingness to control and convert his destructive anger into something more creative, who is to say that he will not go on to follow Roger Federer's winning example? He has certainly shown a willingness to learn from his peers and has admitted: 'You can always learn a lot from watching other players. I am never satisfied with my own performance. There are always areas where I can improve.'

He agrees that one area with room for improvement is his attitude. 'I think to be a consistent player you need to be calm,' Murray has said. 'Federer used to have a pretty bad temper when he was younger but he's addressed the matter. One of the reasons I get annoyed it that I am a perfectionist and right now my tennis is not where I want it to be. I get annoyed when I play bad shots or make stupid mistakes. I think the better I get then the better my temper will be.'

Addressing an occasionally suspect temper was just one of several refinements Murray was encouraged to implement at the end of 2005. One commentator, *The Guardian*'s Stephen Brierly, was even helpful enough to offer Murray his own four-point plan for tennis success. This involved: working harder in training, fighting fatigue, visiting a sports psychologist and thinking 'big' – namely, treating every tournament with the same enthusiasm and vigour as he would Wimbledon – and, finally, 'Forget he is British'. For Brierley, playing like a 'Brit' meant being typecast as the plucky loser. In a tennis world filled with Eastern Europeans, Thais and South Americans who see their sport as the only escape route from poverty – and who are consequently prepared to do anything to succeed – the British attitude of doing it all for the love of the game, win or lose, is simply not good enough.

Following *The Guardian*'s example, there was no shortage of other experts – from the tennis world and beyond – who were not backwards in coming forwards with words of wisdom for Murray. Stewart Ferris, author of *The Little Book of Flirting*, cut straight to the chase. As Murray became richer and more famous, Ferris asserted, so would his appeal to the opposite sex increase in direct proportion. While this was no bad thing, in Ferris's opinion, it did mean that Murray would have to be careful if he chose not to resist the temptations placed in front of him. He commented:

Andy is only 18 and still in short trousers, so he is clearly going to find the forthcoming flood of female attention somewhat bemusing. He'll be wondering if the girls like him for his personality, his looks or for the things he can do with his forehand. The reality is they will be attracted to him because he is a winner. At an instinctive level we are all attracted to people who win: we want to be associated with their success. Andy will have to remember that any girl he talks to should also be treated like a winner. He mustn't take for granted his elevated status and look down on female companions. His aura of celebrity will dissolve once a girl gets to know him, and that's when he'll have to use charm and be romantic like the rest of us.

The signs are that Murray instinctively knows how to handle any speculation about his love life, using humour as his first line of defence. Once, when asked about his romantic arrangements, he quipped: 'I hear that Maria Sharapova fancies me. Only joking. Tell her I'm available, though. Well, sure, girls... they're around, and if there's some time free then there are two or three I might date.' Tellingly, he went on to say: 'But they have to understand what comes first in my life... tennis. And after that... more tennis.' Clearly, Andrew Murray has a highly-developed sense of where his priorities lie.

However, that's not to say that the mask doesn't occasionally slip. When he won his first Tour tournament, in San Jose, USA, in February 2006, an exuberant Murray could not resist celebrating in style by very publicly and very graphically locking lips with his new girlfriend, Kim Sears. Not the sort of behaviour you might expect from the man named at number two in *The Scotsman*'s 2005 Top 50 list of Most Eligible Scottish Batchelors, but

Murray cringes at the thought of having to cut his burgeoning barnet. New girlfriend Kim Sears brought out the scissors in February 2006.

given the circumstances, he can perhaps be forgiven on this occasion.

It certainly is the case that, as his profile grows, Andrew Murray will need to have his media wits about him. If there's one thing the British press loves more than a high-profile winner, it's an ever higher-profile loser. As sure as night follows day, the British press will one day try to tear Murray down with as much gusto and energy as they have spent building him up. The entourage of every major sports star no longer consists of just a trainer and a manager – a PR guru and a rottweiler-like media handler are equally important accessories for successful sportsmen and women these days. As a major new young tennis star picking his way gingerly through the media minefield, Murray's need for help and advice in this area is vital.

In addition to the fame and adulation heading Murray's way, there is, of course, the prospect of enormous wealth. Tennis is not just a sport, it's an immensely lucrative business and its top players can earn millions of pounds in relatively short periods of time. Murray's background is not wealthy by any means and the vast sums of money heading his way cannot but have an effect on his life. On top of the large amounts of prize money on offer, Murray also has the pick of potential sponsors who, like Head and the Royal Bank of Scotland, have already been beating a path to his door.

Despite his immense talent, Murray appears to be the archetypal teenager: bolshie, surly, prone to inexplicable emotional outbursts and sporting the typically adolescent accessories of baseball cap and iPod, as well as a shaggy mane of unkempt hair. He is the sort of boy any teenager can identify with – and that any marketing man would love to have advertising his teen-friendly products.

DVDs, computer games, books: you name it, Andrew Murray has been offered the chance to endorse them. His agent, Sian Masterson, was literally deluged with promotional offers at the end of 2005 once her young charge entered the nation's consciousness. Like any goods agent, Masterson is not prepared to advise Murray to lend his name to any and every product sent his way. But there's no rush: given his age, Murray is expected to reach his peak around 2012, just in time for the London Olympics. The potential rewards for high-profile sportsmen and sportswomen taking part in the biggest sporting event to affect the country since the 1966 World Cup are unimaginable. If Murray were to win the Olympic Men's Tennis gold medal in 2012 his current fame would pale into insignificance. Along with young stars such as the boxer Amir Khan and footballer Wayne Rooney, Murray has the potential to be around for years to come – something sponsors and advertisers are keenly aware of.

'THE MONEY SIDE OF IT NEVER CROSSES MY MIND. SOUNDS CORNY, BUT THAT'S THE TRUTH. WHAT WOULD I SPEND IT ON? A FERRARI? I DON'T THINK SO! DESIGNER SUITS? NO, THANKS! A BIG HOUSE? I DON'T SEE THE SENSE IN OWNING A PLACE WITH MORE ROOMS THAN YOU NEED.'

Andrew Murray on fame and fortune

Yet, despite the commercial feeding frenzy surrounding him, Murray remains refreshingly down-to-earth. 'The money side of it never crosses my mind,' he told one newspaper, adding: 'Sounds corny, but that's the truth. What would I spend it on? A Ferrari? I don't think so. Designer suits? No thanks. A big house? I don't see the sense in owning a place with more rooms than you need.'

Towards the end of 2005, this single-minded young Scot signalled that he was not a pawn to be manipulated in a marketing chess game when he

Both Wayne Rooney and Andy Murray share a huge talent for their sport and a fiery temperament.

elected to leave one of the world's most powerful sports management companies, Octagon, despite protestations from the firm's vice-president Tom Ross, to join up-and-coming Acegroup. In the process, he also rebuffed the attentions of IMG and SFX, two other major heavyweights.

Although Acegroup is much smaller than its rivals, Murray was won over by the organisation's emphasis on placing a high value on an individual's worth and on its purposeful but low profile. They were able to convince Murray that Acegroup would enable him to connect with young people of his own generation and promote tennis as a dynamic, desirable sport in a way that larger, more corporate organisations such as SFX, IMG and Octagon might struggle to do.

Demonstrating that the Acegroup approach was the correct one, in November 2005 Murray had already established himself as a youth figurehead when he launched Raw Tennis, an initiative aimed at eradicating his sport's often stuffy image. Its specific aim was to encourage youngsters from all backgrounds, aged between 10 and 18, to play the game. With its emphasis on making tennis fun (the tricks and flicks usually so reviled by tennis coaches are positively encouraged), Raw Tennis can be played anywhere. Fittingly, Murray launched the scheme in a London car park.

The self-styled youth crusader said he was thrilled at having the opportunity to prove that tennis was not just a sport for the middle classes, the middle-aged and prawn-sandwich chomping toffs. 'It's a thing about British tennis,' he said, 'that people look at it as a middle- to upper-class sport. But with [Raw Tennis] you can play it in the street or the backyard. I really want to promote the programme because it is a really good idea... Growing up, when I saw Wimbledon and I went there, it was all-white and it didn't look that much fun to younger kids. Programmes like this are a really good start for kids and it makes it more fun.'

Murray said he has actively cultivated an image that is instantly accessible to young people, adding: 'The main people who come up to me are the younger kids, who want to have a chat with me. I would much rather have kids come up to me than people who are 40-plus because I want to get more people playing tennis.'

Happily, Murray appears to be a natural when it

> '**I want to be just like Andy. He has got Scottish grit, and I know that because I have played with him. On court he's a bit feisty, but off court he is great. Nothing is going to stop me – I am not a loser at all.'**
>
> Jonny O'Mara, rising Scottish tennis star

comes to speaking for his generation and dealing with the media. He has already developed a trademark approach to interviews that can best be characterised as straightforward and honest. Clearly not a natural diplomat, Murray, in his short career has already gone on record as criticising his opponent Radek Stepanek for gamesmanship following his win over the Czech at Wimbledon. A hefty sideswipe at the LTA (Lawn Tennis Association) for, in his eyes, hindering the career of his brother Jamie also reinforced Murray's Rebel *With* A Cause credentials.

In a sport currently lacking in big personalities, Andrew Murray, with his tell-it-like-it-is approach, has already established himself as a force to be reckoned with. As he himself affirms: 'I said from the start that if there is something which I don't like or believe in I am going to tell everyone. I am not going to tell any lies because I have been brought up not to do that. If someone asks a question to me I will answer it as best as I can.'

One measure of Andrew Murray's success is that he is always referred to as a *British* tennis player, when he is of course Scottish. While he is rightly popular throughout the nation, Andrew Murray is undoubtedly a role model to his fellow Scots, especially in the tennis world.

Ten-year-old Jonny O'Mara is an extravagantly

talented young tennis player from Arbroath, and is being groomed by Andrew Murray's former coach, Leon Smith. In October 2005 he told *The Scotsman*: 'I want to be just like Andy. He has got Scottish grit, and I know that because I have played with him. On court he's a bit feisty, but off court he is great. Nothing is going to stop me. I am not a loser at all.'

Sound familiar?

Another young athlete inspired by Andy is Jade Curtis, Britain's number one girls' tennis player. She admitted: Like everyone else, I've been really impressed by Andy Murray's rankings rise this season. I knew he was a good player but I didn't expect he'd become that good that soon, and I certainly didn't think he'd beat Tim Henman. Tim's always been the top man in British tennis and now it just seems like Andy's taken the spotlight from him. Andy's rise gives me a lot of confidence to know that by being good in the juniors, you can rise quickly in the seniors, too. He's not just played, he's competed well and competed against the likes of Roger Federer. The way he took apart Radek Stepanek on the grass at Wimbledon was phenomenal.

But while we've all been marvelling at the tennis phenomenon that is Andrew Murray, perhaps we should step back and ask ourselves just who this young man is? Where did he come from and what is it that makes Andrew Murray tick?

CHAPTER 2

A TENNIS OBSESSION

ANDREW MURRAY was – and is – a child prodigy. As the history of sport shows, this can be both a blessing and a curse. For every Tiger Woods there is a Diego Maradona. One, a contented and hugely talented golfer, trained from a toddler to be successful; the other an equally gifted footballer driven to the brink of self-destruction by the weight of expectation of an entire nation placed upon him from the earliest age. Who knows which way Andrew Murray will go? Fortunately, the signs look promising. Firstly, although obviously hugely talented from an early age, Murray has only recently entered the spotlight. Unlike Maradona, for example, he was not forced to grow up in public. Second, Andrew Murray appears to be as down-to-earth as they come. Dour even. Definitely more of a Tiger than a Diego.

But this is not to say that it's all been plain sailing for Andy. All the elements of a good old rags-to-riches, young-boy-makes-good story are there: the raw, youthful talent; the intrinsic will to win; the dedicated parent, encouraging the child to make the most of his talent; and the dark cloud of tragedy, haunting the child and spurring him on.

Andrew Barron Murray was born on 15 May, 1987, the second son of Will and Judy Murray. Andrew's older brother, Jamie, had been born the year previously, on 13 February, 1986.

Judy Murray was a former professional tennis player with more than 60 trophies to her name. From 1996 she was also the Scottish national tennis coach. With such a pedigree, it is unsurprising that she wasted no time introducing her two sons to her life-long passion. Andrew in particular showed an early aptitude, and at the age of two, as soon as he could walk, he was already batting balloons and balls around his living room with abandon. Before long, he was taking on his mother and brother at Swingball in the back garden. His path was set.

The next stage in Murray's development came when he graduated on to the tennis courts at his home town of Dunblane. At first, things didn't look promising. 'I'm not sure if I took to it straight away,' he admitted, 'Mum said I wasn't very good.' This is

Dunblane, the town of Andy Murray's birth.

not surprising. His mother was, and is, a hard taskmaster and the four artificial grass courts of Dunblane were not the ideal playing surface. Lashed by wind and rain, they would often dissolve into a muddy quagmire that made any form of tennis impossible.

Nevertheless, by the age of five Murray had not only mastered the fundamentals of tennis, adept at slice and top-spin shots, but had also developed a raging thirst for competition. Recognising this, his mother responded by organising a tennis tournament in Dunblane for Scottish children aged six to nine – including Elena Baltacha, now the British women's number one.

Judy Murray was undoubtedly the driving force behind Andy's early forays into tennis. However, she insists – and her son agrees – that she did not put any undue pressure on him to follow in her footsteps. As far as Judy Murray is concerned, she saw and sensed the innate talent that her son possessed and did everything she could to help him to exploit his natural abilities.

This involved a lot of sacrifice on her part. When Andrew was six, mother and son embarked together on what would be the first of many nationwide road trips, to an under-10 tennis event in Wrexham. She later told *The Daily Telegraph*:

'The event was significant in that it was character building. Each player was guaranteed three one-set matches and Andy lost his first two to much older players. In his final match, played without umpire or court supervisor, and on the furthest court away from the viewing area, he was 6-2 up in the tie-break and was on his way to the net to shake hands after his drop-shot had bounced three times on his opponent's side. His opponent ran forward, smashed the ball back in to the court and claimed the point. Nobody came to help resolve the situation and Andy did not win another point. He was distraught afterwards, but he learnt to stick up for himself after that and has done so ever since.'

'LOSING TO A SIX-YEAR-OLD BOY WAS QUITE EMBARRASSING BUT IN RETROSPECT LOSING TO BRITAIN'S BRIGHTEST NEW TENNIS HOPE IS NOT SO BAD'.

Ryan Openshaw

Clearly, this defeat put some iron in Murray's young soul. That same year he created history at the Waverley Junior Open event in Edinburgh by becoming the youngest winner in the opening round of a Scottish ranking tournament. His opponent, Ryan Openshaw, was 10-years-old. Now a law graduate, Openshaw admits: 'I was a hot favourite to win that

Murray always ensures he stops to sign autographs, remembering how his boyhood hero Andre Agassi didn't provide an autograph for him in 1994.

match because I was four years older than Andrew. No one had ever heard of him. Before he beat me everyone had been talking about his older brother, Jamie, who was also a very promising player. But that soon changed because Andrew made an immediate impression. When you are that young, a four-year gap is massive but even though he was much smaller than me, Andrew won comfortably. Losing to a 6-year-old boy was quite embarrassing but in retrospect losing to Britain's brightest new tennis hope is not so bad.'

While Andrew was acquiring the winning habit, Judy Murray was exploring ways of expanding her son's growing interest in tennis. The answer, naturally, was to take him and a group of other Dunblane children to the Mecca of tennis, Wimbledon, in 1994.

His day out at the home of tennis left an indelible impression on the wide-eyed little boy. The only downside of the visit came when Andre Agassi, Andrew's tennis hero, did not stop to sign his autograph after Murray had spent hours queuing for it. Constantly mindful of his deep disappointment at Agassi's snub, Murray has vowed that he will, unless circumstances make it impossible, stop and sign autographs for any fan that asks for it.

Back home in Dunblane, there inevitably came a time when Andrew Murray's burgeoning interest in tennis began to wane. As with many young boys, football became a big passion for him. Unlike the often lonely and hard-driven slog of tennis, football was a social game, where the burden of responsibility was shared. It was fun, too. Around the ages of seven and eight football became such a focus of Andrew's life that he was courted by Glasgow Rangers. At 11 he was even offered a trial by the

Scottish giants. Sensationally, he turned them down. For one thing, he was a Hibernian supporter (his grandfather, Roy Erskine, played for the Edinburgh club); secondly, by the time he was 11, Andrew was firmly back in the tennis fold.

Andrew Murray can actually remember the precise moment when he realised that tennis was far more important to him than football. He recalled: 'I was practising on [Stirling University tennis courts] and I was supposed to go for football training. My Dad came to collect me and I was just walking off court when I stopped and said, "Forget the football, I'm going back to my tennis training".'

The event that instigated this Road to Damascus moment was a tennis tournament in Solihull, West Midlands. He told the *Sun* journalist Charlie Wyatt: 'My hunger and enthusiasm for tennis was in many ways fired by winning that event in the West Midlands on five consecutive occasions when I was a kid. I won the Under-10s three years in a row when I was eight, nine and 10. I remember being really excited because Jeremy Bates had his name on the Cup – but he only won it once! Then I won the Under-12s at the age of 11 and 12.'

His first overseas event was an under-11 tournament in Rouen, France, where Murray reached the semi-final before losing to French rising star Gaël Monfils, a talented youth who would become not only a regular rival for the Scot in juniors' competition but would also graduate to the senior ranks at the same time as Murray was beginning to establish himself. Thankfully for the Murray family, Jamie exacted due revenge on the Gallic star for his brother's defeat by beating Monfils comprehensively in the final, 6-0 6-1.

Tennis, football, tennis, tennis. Andrew Murray's early years appears to be a golden idyll. But the reality was tragically different. On 13 March, 1996, a terrible event occurred which would have a lasting effect on Murray and which would scar Scotland forever.

Murray was nine years-old when the deranged gunman Thomas Hamilton, an unemployed former shopkeeper and disgraced scout-master, burst into the gymnasium at Dunblane Primary School and massacred 16 children, along with their teacher, Gwen Mayor. He then killed himself.

Both Andrew and his brother Jamie were at school that day, and Andrew was able to escape the bloodbath by hiding in one of the classrooms. In a shocking twist, it emerged that Andrew and Jamie knew Hamilton, as they had both been in his scout group. Once Hamilton's bloody work was done, teachers attempted to calm down their terrified pupils by singing hymns. The events of that terrible day will live on in the memories of those who experienced it forever. In fact, it was only with the passing of time that the full extent of what happened became clear to Andrew, and in 2004 he admitted: 'Because I was so young, I did not understand how big a world event it was. It was not until three or four years ago that I fully realised what had happened and how many people were affected. I was very upset and struggled to understand why it happened. A lot of my classmates lost brothers and sisters, and every family in Dunblane knows somebody affected.'

Jamie Murray still refuses to discuss the incident, but the boys' mother perhaps echoes the thoughts and feelings of many parents when she says in the *Daily Telegraph*, 'I don't want to sound corny but, because there are no words to really explain what everyone went through, all I can say is that it was the worst day of my life; you could never, ever have imagined anything like that happening in your little, peaceful village... never. Andy was 8 and his big brother, Jamie, 9. I had a shop at the time in the heart of Dunblane selling toys and children's clothes – so I knew just about everyone involved, if only by sight – and someone burst in to say there was a man found dead with a gun in the playground. I ran out the shop, crashed into my mum – who was coming in to tell me – got in the car and drove like the furies, yelling "GET OUT OF MY WAY!" at every driver. It was hours later that Jamie and Andy finally appeared. I hugged them, bundled them into the car and it was only then I appreciated how wonderful the teachers had been. The boys had been given lunch and all they knew was that a man had been in the school with a gun. They'd no idea what had actually happened. Every member of staff knew exactly what had occurred and for them to protect our children from the enormity of it all was incredible. I stopped the car and explained everything as gently as I could.'

While it is difficult to look for positive outcomes in such a dreadful tragedy, it is the case that Andrew Murray somehow tries to draw on the experiences of that terrible day to motivate himself even now. He explains: 'Dunblane has coped really well with getting itself back on its feet, but it is still known around the world for the wrong reasons. I would like to think I am bringing some hope to everyone in Dunblane and also putting it in the headlines for the right reasons.'

A more positive driving force in Andrew's early career was the fierce sibling rivalry he developed with Jamie. When Jamie and Andrew were four and three respectively they were already attempting to outdo each other on the tennis court. Andrew confessed that: 'He beat me every time. Then he would brag about it all week, which used to drive me crazy. He was bigger and stronger than me, but I just worked and worked and pushed myself harder – all the time my dream was to beat him, and that has made me more competitive.'

> '**I hate losing. I don't play tournaments to come second best,'**
> Andrew Murray

While the Murray boys were slogging it out on court, Judy Murray was always standing on the sidelines, urging her sons on, honing their intensely competitive spirits. And that's not where Judy Murray's influence ends; Andrew also believes that he has inherited his mother's fierce temper. As a Taurean, he also feels that it is perhaps written in the stars that he is prone to bullish and sometimes petulant behaviour.

Sibling rivalry spurred Andrew on to greater heights, though here he's partnering older brother Jamie.

As a youngster, Andrew found it difficult to control his rages. Many a racket was destroyed during a Murray temper tantrum. Things got so bad that Judy Murray would eventually confiscate her son's rackets as punishment for any bouts of bad behaviour. In normal life, such petulance would win a person few friends, but in tennis it is indicative of a passionate desire to win – a prerequisite for anyone who wants to get ahead in the ultra-competitive world of sport. 'I hate losing,' Murray readily admits. 'I don't play any tournaments to come second best.' Coming from a British sports star, this sounds almost revolutionary.

'ANDY IS ONE OF THOSE GIFTED INDIVIDUALS THAT COME ALONG EVERY SO OFTEN',

Leon Smith, Andrew's first coach

Driven on by his insatiable will to win, Andrew Murray quickly learned all he could about tennis from his mother. Judy Murray, knowing that her son needed more teaching and attention than she would be able to give, hired the 21-year-old Glaswegian Leon Smith to coach and mentor the 11-year-old Andrew. Smith remembers: 'It began with individual lessons, and the two of us got on really well. Andy is one of those gifted individuals that come along every so often. He has good genes, and enthusiasm. I remember when I was playing as a junior he would be there watching, and he was only three years old at the time. More importantly, on and off the court, even as an 11-year-old he was very competitive whether it was playing cards, board games or table tennis.' Over the next four years Smith would help Andrew to lift his game to unimaginable heights, moving him from the ranks of promising beginners to potential stars of the future.

The first fruits of the Murray-Smith partnership appeared in 1999, Andrew's first really successful year as a new star in the tennis firmament. In addition to winning the Junior British National Championship at Under-12 level, Andrew endeared himself to French fans by twice winning tournaments there – in Auray and Aguen.

However, in order for Murray to be deemed an unqualified success he had to 'crack' America, which he duly did in spectacular style when he triumphed in Florida's 12 and Under Orange Bowl Tournament, an unofficial world championships for young people. Future greats such as Andre Agassi and Jim Courier had all previously won the Orange Bowl Tournament. Murray's victory there in 1999 truly made tennis watchers sit up and take

Like Andy Murray, Andre Agassi was a winner at the Orange Bowl Tournament in Florida. But will Andy also hold the Wimbledon trophy aloft one day?

notice of the young Scot, especially as he was only the second British male, after Jamie Delgado, to lift the trophy. The fact that Murray defeated the world junior number one, Tomas Pistacek of the Czech Republic, on his way to taking the title only served to enhance his growing reputation.

Discussing his victory afterwards, Andrew revealed: '[My opponent] hits a lot of winners and he also misses a lot. I figured that I'd get the ball back and when I have a chance to go for it I would and it worked.' This strategy of consistently accurate returning and waiting for his opponent to make errors was to prove a favoured Murray tactic in years to come.

Around this time, Andrew also began to hone his doubles skills, first with his brother and then with fellow talented British youngster, Tom Rushby, from Derby. In December 2000, Rushby and Murray teamed up to win the Under-14 Prince Cup in the USA, following the Scot's singles success in the same competition. The following year, Murray teamed up with Surrey's Andrew Kennaugh to secure the Windmill Cup in Holland, and two months later the Murray-Kennaugh pairing combined to win the Under-15 British Junior Championships, where Murray also achieved victory in the singles.

By 2002, as the singles and doubles titles mounted up, it was clear that Murray's abilities needed to be tested further. He had literally outgrown Scotland and the opportunities and competition it had to offer. Patrice Hagelauer, the Lawn Tennis Association's director of performance, insisted that Murray would have to leave his homeland if wanted to develop further and advised him to move to the LTA academy in Loughborough.

Andrew was not so keen. In 1998 his brother spent what had been a tortuous and difficult eight-month spell at the LTA's school in Cambridge. In 1998 Jamie had been a very promising, up-and-coming youngster, often mentioned in the same breath as Spain's Rafael Nadal and Richard Gasquet of France. Following his stint at the LTA's school, any enthusiasm that Jamie Murray once had for tennis was swiftly and brutally eroded through a combination of debilitating homesickness and what he considered to be unhelpful tampering with his technique. Andrew was later to lambast the LTA for its treatment of Jamie, saying: 'My brother is very talented. He was number two in the world when he was around the age of 13 and then he went down to an LTA in Cambridge and they ruined him for a few years. It was their fault.'

Unsurprisingly, Andrew Murray decided not to put himself in the care of the LTA. Instead, he decided to continue his quest for tennis excellence abroad. In Spain.

CHAPTER 3

VIVA ESPANA

IN SEPTEMBER 2002 Andrew Murray arrived at Barcelona's Sánchez-Casal Open Sports Club tennis academy. It was here, in what would become his second home, that Andrew Murray would hone and refine his tennis skills to become the player that he is today.

Run by former Spanish Davis Cup stalwarts Emilio Sánchez and Sergio Casal, the Open Sports Club lies in a sumptuous setting between two natural parks, offering more than 100,000 square metres of leafy greenery, top-class training facilities and exemplary coaching and education. In tennis terms, it is a veritable paradise, a place where someone as consumed with the game as Murray can live, breathe, eat and sleep tennis.

It is frightening to imagine that Murray very nearly didn't join the Open Sports Club, and that it was only a life-changing conversation with rising Spanish star and junior contemporary Rafael Nadal in February 2002 that convinced Andrew to decamp to Spain. Following Spain's 2-1 win over Britain in the European Under-16 team championships in Andorra, Nadal and Murray set aside their national allegiances and went for a game of squash. As they played they discussed their respective training routines – and Murray was both alarmed and enthused by the marked contrast between Nadal's tennis education and his own.

The Scot lamented that he was becoming increasingly frustrated by the lack of playing

Murray swapped the rain and the cold of his homeland for sun-kissed Spain in 2002.

partners of comparable ability to his own country, by the fact that schoolwork often took precedence over his sporting passion, and by the irritating vagaries of the British weather which seriously hampered tennis practice. Nadal, meanwhile, waxed lyrical about how he, in a purpose-built academy in Majorca, could spend most of the year playing tennis outside in brilliant sunshine with older and more experienced campaigners such as Carlos Moya, in addition to receiving a first-class education.

Judy Murray reveals that: 'Andy came home and went absolutely bananas. He said, "They're training for hours against top-quality players and who have I got to hit with – my brother!" He was at an academy in Scotland, but to be honest, it was not the right environment for him.' Murray was determined to experience the same top-level tennis tuition as Nadal and, with his mother, set about researching the world's top tennis academies.

Swayed perhaps by the enticing vision of Spain as a tennis wonderland that Nadal had sold to him, Andrew eventually chose the Sánchez-Casal academy as his favoured destination. But would the academy have Andrew? Any doubts on that front were soon dispelled when Murray thrashed co-owner Sánchez, winner of 15 ranking tennis titles, 6-1 6-3 during a practice match.

With the tennis school selected, the next issue

what how to raise the £25,000-£30,000 fees necessary to pay for it. Thankfully, and despite Murray's low opinion of them, the LTA, together with Tennis Scotland and Sport Scotland, provided most of the money. Family funds and private sponsorship made up the rest.

> 'I chose to go to Spain because I thought it would mean harder work and be better for my tennis.'
>
> Andrew Murray

Turning his back on his country was not a decision Murray arrived at lightly. He was leaving behind his family, friends and all the familiarities of life in Britain for a completely new existence in Spain. Andrew's move to Spain was not just a personal decision; it was also a well-aimed sock in the eye for the LTA.

A recurring theme throughout Andrew Murray's career has been his unabashed criticism of the LTA. In his view, the LTA panders to the worst instincts of British tennis: self-satisfied and stuffy, it over-protects and pampers British tennis stars well beyond the level that their achievements merit. Meanwhile, young players and emerging talents are left to potter along with no real support or direction.

Even at the age of 15 Andrew was acutely aware that the dearth of emerging players in British tennis to replace old warhorses such as Tim Henman and

Greg Rusedski was a damning indictment of what he perceived as the lackadaisical attitude to sport in Britain. 'Down in London, I think the young players tend to get a little bit spoilt,' Murray told *The Sunday Times*. 'I chose to go to Spain because I thought it would mean harder work and be better for my tennis.' Following on from this, he later claimed: 'One of the problems in Britain I think is that they don't give sport enough attention and that's why there have not been any great [British] sportsmen in the last 10 years. When I moved over to Spain, they've been great, they take tennis as my priority and actually help me a lot.'

> **'THE BOTTOM LINE IS, YOU DON'T NEED TO BE A ROCKET SCIENTIST TO BE GOOD AT TENNIS,'**
>
> Andrew Murray

While he was in the mood to take on the Establishment, the young Scot then turned his fire on the British education system: 'I have no regrets even if it was a wrench to leave everything behind at 15. We've created this culture where you have to study biology, physics... Why? Frankly, I don't believe it is important for somebody such as myself, who wants to be the best at tennis, to be the best at biology, just as you wouldn't insist that every would-be doctor

Andrew trained against the likes of a personal hero, Guillermo Coria.

was also a red-hot golfer or runner... The bottom line is you don't need to be a rocket scientist to be good at tennis.'

He may not be a rocket scientist, but Andrew Murray is no fool either. One very real benefit of removing himself to Spain from Britain was that it left him free to develop his skills in peace, away from the media frenzy at home where the search for a successor to Tim Henman as British number one would inevitably erupt as 'Tiger' Tim's time at the top came to an end.

Instead, the only pressure that Andrew would be

subjected to would be that put on him by himself and his teachers. And what pressure it was. Spain seems to have perfected the art of producing clay-court gladiators, capable of returning the ball with metronome-like regularity and cannon-like power. Every day on court for Andrew was like undergoing an aerial bombardment, launched from the opposite baseline with unerring accuracy by the likes of Carlos Moya and Andrew's hero, Guillermo Coria. It was all to the good, though, as he readily admits:

Emilio Sanchez (left) co-ran an academy in Spain at which Andrew Murray started in September 2002.

'I think practising in Spain helped me a lot because I got to play with senior players all the time. You get used to how hard they're hitting the ball. And it helped me to know where I should be hitting the ball when I'm playing matches. That's one of the reasons why I think I can make it.'

The fact that he was perfecting his craft on clay courts was also important to Murray. He argues that, 'You have to be able to play well on clay to get anywhere in tennis,' adding: 'The only problem is that there's no clay courts in the UK so I had to go to Spain.' He also perceived another benefit in moving abroad, claiming: 'The mental side to my game has improved by being in Spain as well. On clay you can't afford to miss any balls so I think my mental toughness is getting much better.'

But it wasn't all work, work, work. Given such a punishing schedule, it was important that students at the academy learned to enjoy their time there. One thing the school prides itself on is the sense of camaraderie it promotes among its students. The international tennis tour can be a gruelling experience where you need all the friends you can get, even if these same friends are also your rivals. It was certainly a positive sign that when Andrew won the US Open Juniors' title in 2004 one of his friends from the academy, the Russian Svetlana Kuznetsova, was cheering him on from the sidelines.

Daily life at the Sanchez and Casal academy consisted of a carefully-planned round of tennis training, exerting exercise routines and intensive mental coaching, so that the needs of the mind as well as the body were catered for.

The day would usually begin with two-and-a-half hours of tennis practice under the watchful eyes of Sergio Casal, Angel Gimenez, Antonio Hernandez and supervised by Emilio Sánchez-Vicario. This was followed by one-and-a-half hours of physical conditioning before the daily mental toughness coaching of Dr. Jorge Valverde. On top of all this, there was also three hours of academic education each day, during which Murray studied French, English, Maths and colloquial Spanish.

In this rigorous regime, each player's strengths and weaknesses were quickly identified and worked on. In Murray's case, one particular flaw that came under close scrutiny was his combustibility. This was quickly – though not entirely – ironed out by pitching the surly young Caledonian in against seasoned old hands, who treated Andrew's tantrums with the amused contempt that they deserved. Murray soon learned to control his anger and then channel it in a more positive direction.

The power of positive thinking came in useful in other ways, too. Given his youthfulness and his

Andy's mother has always been a constant
source of support for him.

closeness to his family, it is not unreasonable to expect Andrew to have experienced some degree of homesickness. However, he seemed to genuinely enjoy his time in Spain. True, regular visits from his mother – laden down with treats, such as chocolate digestive biscuits – helped Andrew to retain a link with his native land, but he never experienced the debilitating pining for home that many of his contemporaries did.

Instead, Andrew thrived in the multinational, multicultural atmosphere of the academy – which proved to be the perfect preparation for life on the international tennis circuit.

Spartan would perhaps best describe conditions at the academy. Students were not pampered and cosseted; instead, they were housed in boarding school-style accommodation. At one point, Andrew was sharing a cramped wooden bungalow, complete with bunk beds, with a teenage Ukrainian.

A reporter sent out from *The Daily Telegraph* to interview Murray describes the scene: 'The floor was smothered with a week's worth of discarded rackets, clay-stained shorts, used tennis balls and empty crisp packets. This could have been your average teenager's bedroom. "You should have seen it this morning," said his mother, Judy. "I could hardly open the door. I've had a bit of a tidy-up".'

And while his mother was cleaning up his room,

Andrew was cleaning up on the court, winning tournament after tournament in quick succession.

In October 2002 he won both the singles and doubles of the Torneig ITF Andorra La Vella tournament. This was followed in January 2003 by the Pony Malta Cup, in which he defeated Leanardo Kirche from Brazil in the final. That same year Andrew also won the Canadian Open crown, the 11th International Junior Tournament 'Citta Di Prato' title in Italy and the Nottingham ITF junior trophy.

In addition to a handful of successes in doubles tournaments – he also reached the semi-final of Junior Wimbledon with Tom Rushby – Murray also demonstrated his pedigree in the United States, reaching the quarter-finals of the US Open Juniors before losing 6-1 7-5 to Romanian second seed Florin Mergea. But despite all of this international success a definite highlight for Andrew came in September, when he beat several experienced senior players in a Futures event in Glasgow on the way to becoming the youngest-ever Briton to win a £10,000 tournament prize – in his home country of Scotland, to boot.

If 2003 ended well for Murray, 2004 started badly as he was sidelined by a knee injury – attributed to a growth spurt – that kept him sidelined for eight months. It was especially frustrating as Andrew

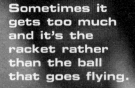

Sometimes it gets too much and it's the racket rather than the ball that goes flying.

was at the time rated as the second best junior in world tennis, behind France's Gael Monfils.

By now, Murray was being looked after full-time by his boyhood coach, Leon Smith, who supported the youngster during his rehabilitation period back in Scotland. Smith recalls: 'When we did decided to go full-time, unfortunately he got his knee injury, and the next seven months were very difficult. I would pick him up every single day, go to the gym at Stirling, then go and play snooker at Bridge of Allan, and then do some swimming. It was a difficult time.'

When back in his homeland, Murray was a visitor to Edinburgh's Craiglockart tennis and sports centre where former employee Ruth Nickson remembers his impressive work ethic and commitment to training.

'He used to practise for hours,' she said. 'You could see that he had the talent to become something special.'

When Murray eventually returned to action in the summer of 2004 he quickly confirmed that he was still a force to be reckoned with in spectacular style by winning the US Open Juniors. Later that year, he collected two more titles on Spanish soil, in Pontevedra and Orense respectively, as his days as a junior drew to a close.

Murray was now being coached by the hugely experienced Colombian, Pato Alvarez, who had guided more than 40 Top 50 players, including Gustavo Kuerten. When he took him under his wing, Pato declared that he had never seen a more luminous talent than Murray. The next stage in Andrew Murray's unstoppable rise was about to begin.

CHAPTER 4

AMERICAN DREAM

THE US Open is typically American in its awe-inspiring size, brashness and relentless noise and razzmatazz. Surely all the gaudy glitz and glamour would be too much for a young lad from provincial Scotland? Not a bit of it; Andrew Murray simply adores the US Open and everything it represents: the floodlit night matches and the rock 'n' roll ambience make this tournament in particular a festival of fun for tennis's brat pack, of which Murray is a fully paid up member.

And it seems that Murray's affection for the US Open is more than reciprocated. When he took the 2004 junior tournament by storm, going on to win it, the fans were completely won over by the passionate young unknown and he quickly became a crowd favourite.

Prior to the tournament Murray was seeded

number three, with junior world number one Gaël Monfils the favourite. Yet the Frenchman was a surprise casualty at the quarter-final stage. Murray, meanwhile, was in imperious form as he romped through the draw, losing just one set in the process. Argentina's Juan Del Potro was swept aside 6-0, 6-1 in the first round, with local boy Vahid Mirzadeh disposed of 6-1, 6-2 in the next round. New Zealand's Will Ward was then accounted for 6-1, 6-2, before another American, wildcard Sam Querrey, provided Murray with his stiffest test yet. Losing the first set 6-2, Murray proved his pugnacious nature by taking the next two sets 7-6, 6-1 and securing a place in the semi-final.

France's Gaël Monfils was a keen rival of Murray's when the pair were juniors.

One of Murray's greatest achievements to date as he holds aloft the US Open junior trophy.

His 6-3 6-2 semi-final win over the German Mihail Zverev was a bittersweet occasion, as it came just after Murray and his brother were defeated in the doubles semi-finals by Brendan Evans and Scott Oudsema of the USA. Surprisingly, Murray's anger at this loss exceeded his joy at winning a place in the singles final. At the end of the doubles match he stormed off the court and refused to shake hands with the umpire. Once he had calmed down Murray confessed: 'I was really disappointed because I felt I had let my brother down. It was a really big occasion for him and my mum as well. If we'd both got to a Grand Slam final that would have been the best thing for her – it was her birthday earlier on in the week.' Jamie generously reminded his brother that if it hadn't been for Andrew they would never have reached the semi-final in the first place. Reassured, Andrew resolved to make sure he would not lose the singles final.

'I DON'T PLAY TO COME SECOND.'

Andrew Murray

Considering that he was the first British male to reach the final of the boys' singles since 1973, Murray was remarkably cool before the match. He went so far as to say: 'Obviously I'd like to win it now – I don't play to come second. It's a great achievement to get to a Grand Slam final but it's only juniors. I'd prefer to do it in the seniors.'

Andrew's cool confidence was surely boosted by the identity of his opponent, the Ukrainian Sergiy Stakhovsky. Murray had already played him several times at Under-14 level and beaten him with consummate ease. Sure enough, Andrew was able to dispose of Stakhovsky 6-4 6-2 in just 95 minutes, hammering down two aces in the process and making 61 per cent of his first serves.

'I'm a little bit surprised to win, but not too much.'
Andrew Murray plays it cool after winning the 2004 US Open juniors' title

In winning the US Open boys' singles title Andrew Murray joined a select group of players. First off, he

Murray thrashes
Stakhovsky 6-4
6-2 to capture
the US Open
boys' singles
crown, the first
Briton to win a
junior Grand Slam
title since 1993.

became the first British winner of the US Open boys' singles and the first from his country to secure a Grand Slam since James Baily won the Australian Open juniors in 1993. Second, he also joined the likes of Pat Cash, Stefan Edberg and Andy Roddick in the illustrious roll-call of former champions.

In victory, Murray was in tell-it-like-it-is mode, opting for honesty rather than fake modesty. After citing his own long-term injury worries from earlier in the year, he confessed: 'I'm a little bit surprised to win, but not too much. I played four warm-up tournaments in Spain and Italy before, senior tournaments, and I'd won two of them playing really well. I think the competition in those tournaments was stronger than what it was here. I felt like I could win the tournament, but I wasn't really expecting to.' This is not how British sports stars are *supposed* to speak and Murray's uncompromising honesty was, if nothing else, a breath of fresh air in the often stuffy world of British mens' tennis.

If Murray seemed distinctly underwhelmed by his victory, he was clearly more enthusiastic about the US Open as a tournament. 'Well, this is my favourite tournament,' he gushed uncharacteristically. 'I just think the atmosphere, all of the matches that I played here, was really good. You know, the fans are great. I think the night matches here are just really good for the supporters. I'd love to come back and hopefully play a night match one time. But to play here, I think it's the biggest tournament in the world.' This last remark undoubtedly raised a few eyebrows at the LTA and at Wimbledon, but it clearly demonstrated that Murray was only interested in saying what he wanted to say and not what he was expected to say. Among impressed onlookers was Murray's grandfather, Roy Erskine, who told BBC Sport, 'I watched the game by looking at the score point-by-point on the internet.'

Yet once the hype and euphoria had subsided, the inevitable question was asked: was he the 'real deal' or just a flash in the pan?

For every Tim Henman or Greg Rusedski, genuinely successful British tennis players, there is a James Baily or a Martin Lee, youthful bright sparks who were unable to translate their talent into the senior professional ranks. Which way would Murray go?

'WE'VE HAD PLENTY OF EXAMPLES OF KIDS THAT HAVE DONE WELL IN THE JUNIORS BUT HAVEN'T MADE THAT TRANSITION. BUT NOT ONLY HIS GAME, BUT BETWEEN THE EARS, ANDREW KNOWS WHAT HE'S DOING. HE WORKS HARD AND I THINK THAT'S A GOOD COMBINATION.'

Tim Henman

One person who thinks that Andrew Murray has what it takes to succeed is Tim Henman himself. 'We've had plenty of examples of kids that have done well in the juniors but haven't made that transition,' he says. 'But not only his game, but between the ears, Andrew knows what he's doing. He works hard and I think that's a good combination.'

Others have pointed out that Henman was never a great player as a junior, and that he owed a large part of his success to his intense determination to improve, to the hours he spent working on his game. Starting from a higher base of natural ability, they claim that Murray shows as much desire and determination – more in fact – than Henman and can only go on to bigger and better things.

Writing in the *Daily Telegraph*, Sue Mott urged caution, pointing out that it benefited no one to hail Murray as the new saviour of British tennis so early in his career: 'He can probably cope – his mother, Judy, is formidable – but it would be kinder to all concerned to let him continue his sunny development without the demands of being Jonny Wilkinson, Francis of Assisi and Hellboy all rolled into one.' Wise words – but a lot easier said than done.

Annabel Croft, who won the Wimbledon women's juniors title aged 17, knew exactly what lay in store for Murray. Once the glamour of his first big tournament faded, she warned him that he faced a long, hard slog in attempting to consolidate his growing reputation in a series of lesser tournaments around the world. She cautioned: 'Suddenly you realise that you are hot property. Everyone wants a piece of you: the sponsors, the coaches, the agents. But there is a massive wake up call on the Tour because you are playing to such a high level every single day. It's a huge mental battle more than anything. While the superstars of the game fly first class to the glamour spots around the globe, those on the first rung of the ladder travel economy, live cheaply and fight tooth and nail for every ranking point. You get to the satellite events and you are there at 7:00 a.m. to sign in for pre-qualifying because your ranking is so low that you can't even get in to qualifying, then every match you play is like the final of the junior championship you have just won.'

Clearly, success had its downsides – but it had it upsides, too. And given the choice between having to deal with failure and having to deal with success,

Andrew Murray was going to choose the former. His win at the US Open proved that he was ready for anything.

Murray's grandparents Roy and Shirley Erskine celebrate his US Open win. Roy watches his grandson's progress live on the internet.

CHAPTER 5

TURNING PRO

FEW PLAYERS in the game, past and present, have the kind of charisma and appeal that speaks to tennis fans across the generations. John McEnroe is one such player. He's the kind of man you want on your side, and you certainly would not want him as an enemy. Imagine Andrew's surprise, then, when in October 2004 McEnroe not only declared himself an out-and-out fan of the teenage prodigy – he even offered to coach him on a part-time basis. As McEnroe himself once said: 'You cannot be serious!'

As Andrew Murray's junior career drew to a close, things suddenly began to move. The event that propelled him towards the big league was the Superset tennis tournament, held at Wembley Arena, London, in October 2004. The brainchild of Australian entrepreneur Steve Duval, Superset was an unashamed tennis jamboree. Eight players, past and present, were invited along to play each other in exciting, one-set, sudden-death face-offs. It was the sort of event that tennis purists hate and fans and spectators love. Adding some extra spice to the mix was the not inconsiderable £250,000 prize money.

Luminaries including Tim Henman, Greg Rusedski, Goran Ivanisevic and Mario Ancic were invited to take part, as was John McEnroe himself. There was no way a virtual unknown such as Andrew Murray would be asked to compete, too, would there? Well no – but fate had other plans. When Tim Henman pulled out of the extravaganza at the last minute with a shoulder injury, Andrew Murray was asked to step into the breech.

'I'M SO EXCITED TO PLAY MCENROE, HE'S SOMEBODY I LOOKED UP TO WHEN I WAS YOUNGER AND A REAL LEGEND,'

Andrew Murray at the Superset tennis tournament,
October 2004

The prospect of playing against McEnroe (career earnings: £7 million) was the thing that really excited Murray (career earnings: £7,317). He told the media: 'I'm really pumped to play an event like Superset Tennis and to have the opportunity to play with some of the greatest players ever. I'm so excited to play McEnroe, he's somebody I looked up to when I was younger and a real legend.' Of course, fairy tales don't always come true and McEnroe, the 45-year-old seasoned sorcerer, handed out a ruthless tennis lesson to his 17-year-old opponent, beating him 6-1.

McEnroe's highly polished, lethal serve-and-volley game was a brutal reminder of his wonderful

McEnroe hammers Murray 6-1 at the Albert Hall in October 2004.

past as he obliterated the Scot in just 24 minutes. An awe-struck Murray could only muster the following response to the mastery of his opponent: 'I learned a lot and I got to play one of the greatest players of all time. He may not be as good as he used to be, but he's still pretty good.' Note, of course, the uncompromising honesty in Murray's 'may not be as good as he used to be' remark.

The wily McEnroe offered words of comfort to his defeated opponent after the game: 'I feel like I smothered him before he got a chance to get into it. He looks like he's got the potential to be a good player but he needs to get used to situations like this.' McEnroe was quite right. As Supermac milked the crowd, Murray stood to one side, flanked by two leggy blondes and grinning nervously. Clearly, there was more to grown-up tennis than just hitting the ball over the net.

For Murray, defeat at the hands of McEnroe was painful. The Superset tournament may have essentially been a bit of fun, but the simple fact is that he hates to lose, no matter what. The tournament had also raised his profile – but perhaps not in the way he would have wanted, when he was seen to be just another one off the production line of plucky British losers, anonymous cannon fodder for the crowd-pleasing McEnroe. Everything about Andrew Murray's game was directed towards winning at all costs, at transforming the way that British tennis players were seen by the world. He didn't want to go out like this and had to show that he possessed that quality intrinsic to all sporting heroes: bouncebackability.

But before Murray could begin to rebuild his confidence he discovered that his body had not quite finished building him. An untimely growth spurt at the beginning of 2005 (at one point Murray was growing by a centimetre a week) placed an enormous amount of stress on Andrew's frame and he was hit by a debilitating back injury.

After missing a couple of Challenger tournaments in both South America and Europe, Murray was only able to return to action in March – where he made a dazzling debut appearance for Britain's Davis Cup team against Israel. He then resumed singles action at the Barletta Challenger clay court event in Italy, where he reached the second round before being beaten in two sets by France's Arnaud Di Pasquale, 6-4 6-3. His next outing, in early April on the hard courts of Cremona in Italy, was more fruitful as he made the semi-finals of the Futures tournament, before losing out to Ireland's Kevin Sorensen, 3-6 4-6. Slowly but surely, Andrew was working his way back to full fitness and form.

Just in time, too, because his next match would

Murray can count on some high-profile friends on the tennis circuit, including the 2004 US Open women's champion, Svetlana Kuznetsova who trains with him in Spain

mark Andrew Murray's professional debut on the ATP tour. Fittingly, it took place in Barcelona, his adopted home, the city where one of the daily sports papers welcomed him back with the headline: 'El futuro del tenis Britanico'. In front of many of his tennis friends and fans, including 2004 US Open women's champion Svetlana Kuznetsova, the 17-year-old ace made an impressive start against the Czech Jan Hernych, breaking him twice to take the first set 6-3.

He subsequently showed his strength of character in the second set, breaking back to level at 4-4, before his opponent broke again to restore parity and take the match to a deciding set. As the action and the tension mounted Murray suddenly fell victim to cramp. It would not be the last time he would suffer this cruel affliction in the early days of his professional career. It was a sign that while Murray's spirit was willing his flesh was still relatively weak. At 17, he was still growing and developing, and sometimes, the more he pushed it to new limits, his body just said 'no'.

Battling through the pain, the big-hearted Scot forced his way into a 3-1 lead before mistakes on key points led to his downfall. Hernych broke back twice to earn the third set and match, 6-4.

It was an immensely encouraging first appearance for Murray in the professional arena, and he could be extremely pleased that he often produced the more accomplished tennis against a man ranked 79 in the world, well above Murray's lowly ranking of 393. 'I've got a very good chance to get to the top,' Andrew commented afterwards. 'I'm only 17 and this guy was about 75 in the world. I didn't play well at all today. I need to improve my physical strength because that let me down a bit toward the end of the third set.'

Murray's coach, Pato Alvarez, was an extremely proud man, believing the tenacity and flair his charge had shown for large chunks of the match augured well for the future. He explained: 'This is his first main serious competition at this level and he had about 10 or 11 break points. The only problem was nerves. He just needs to play more and have the mentality to believe he can win, which he will develop over the next year. When he arrived here, he was used to a different style and so was making many mistakes.' Alvarez went on to say that there was no doubt in his mind that Murray would eliminate these mistakes from his game. As for developing a winning mentality – there was definitely no problem there. Little did Alvarez know at that point that Murray would go on to make a name for himself on the ATP tour in the ensuing months – but without his help.

'I JUST WASN'T ENJOYING THINGS ON OR OFF THE COURT. HE WAS TRYING TO GET ME TO PLAY IN A WAY I DIDN'T LIKE AND IT JUST WASN'T WORKING.'

Andrew Murray on sacking his coach,
Pato Alvarez

Shortly afterwards, Murray sacked the 69-year-old Colombian, demonstrating a steely single-mindedness in the way he wanted to play tennis. He was typically forthright in his explanation for removing his coach: 'I just wasn't enjoying things on or off the court. He was trying to get me to play in a way I didn't like and it just wasn't working. He wanted me to be less aggressive and play more like the Spanish players. That's not the way I play – I like to play hard.'

The age difference between Alvarez and Murray may also have played a part. Coach and player live in close proxmimity to each other during the ceaseless exertions of the tennis tour. If the pair have similar ages and interests it helps to while away the hours off the court. Being more akin to grandfather and grandson, it would have been very difficult for Murray and Alvarez to have bonded meaningfully.

Once Murray made his decision, things very quickly turned sour. He later revealed: 'The last week we were together it got a bit nasty. He was saying some bad things about my tennis and bad things about me. I don't really need someone that negative in my corner.' In April 2006, Alvarez's successor as Murray's coach, Mark Petchey, also parted company with his charge.

With no coaching support – save his ever-present mother, Judy – Murray struggled for consistency in his next few tournaments. A semi-final appearance in a Futures tournament in Lleida, Spain, where he lost 7-5, 7-5 to the Spaniard Javier Genaro-Martinez, was followed by an early exit from the next Futures event in Vic at the start of May, losing 6-4, 6-3 to another Spaniard, Daniel Gimeno-Traver. In mid-May, Switzerland's Michael Lammer knocked Murray out of the Challenger event in Dresden, Germany, winning 6-4, 6-3 in their second-round clash.

> **'The last week we were together it got a bit nasty. He was saying some bad things about my tennis and bad things about me. I don't really need someone that negative in my corner.'**
>
> Andrew Murray on his former coach, Pato Alvarez

Later in the month he sought to add a second consecutive junior Grand Slam to his collection when he travelled to France to take part in the French Open. Murray was installed as top seed for the event at Roland Garros in Paris, a welcome fillip to the youngster following months of irritating injury niggles and coaching departures.

However, Murray nearly fell at the first hurdle after a tough battle with Venezuela's Piero Luisi, from which the resilient Scot finally emerged victorious, 6-4 2-6 6-3. Straight-set victories ensued from then on as Murray earned a showdown with an emerging Croatian, Marin Cilic, in the semi-final. Unfortunately, the Scot's irascible temper got the better of him during the game. At one point Murray was serving for the first set. Cilic managed to hang on and eventually won the set himself. Murray, intensely self-critical, lost his self-belief and slumped to a straight-sets defeat. Along the way he mangled a couple of his own tennis rackets, cursed freely and generally moped about like a surly teenager on the verge of being sent to his room. He even picked up a code violation for one particularly violent bout of racket abuse, and was coded again *after* Cilic had converted match point, again for destroying his racket.

To make matters worse, Murray and fellow Brit Andrew Kennaugh's dreams of Grand Slam glory in the doubles competition were also thwarted when they succumbed at the quarter-final stage to Russians Pavel Chekhov and Valeri Rudnev. In a fiercely-contested tussle, the Russians finally triumphed 8-6 in the third set after the first two were shared 6-4 1-6.

A measure of consolation to soothe Murray's double dose of disappointment arrived with the news that he had been given a wildcard for June's Wimbledon warm-up series, the Stella Artois tournament.

'GRASS ISN'T MY FAVOURITE SURFACE,'

Andrew Murray commits heresy in the run-up to the 2005 Stella Artois Tournament

In fact, with this news, Murray managed to turn his defeat into a positive, claiming that it meant he would not be saddled with any ridiculous expectations for the British grass-court season as he might have been had he secured a second Grand Slam title. 'If I'd won the title all that would have happened is that I would have had 10 times more pressure on me,' he argued. 'So when I look at it like that maybe it's a good thing. Maybe everyone will have slightly lower expectations over the next few weeks during the grass court season, especially as grass isn't my favourite surface.'

The Stella Artois tournament at Queen's Club in London is viewed as the ideal preparation for Wimbledon for many of the world's top players. Following his French Open exploits, Murray only had a day-and-a-half's practice on grass before Queen's, taking part in an exhibition match with Mario Ancic at Surbiton. Thankfully, his first-round opponent, Santiago Ventura, was, on paper, an easy opener for Murray as he attempted to make a rapid transition from clay to grass. Ranked at 110 in the world, Ventura was actually playing his first-ever match on grass. It showed, as he struggled to cope with Murray's arsenal of heavy serves, powerful ground strokes and decisive final volleys.

> **'A few of the shots he produced in that match some of us can only dream of,'**
>
> Mark Petchey on Andrew Murray, following his win against Taylor Dent at the 2005 Stella Artois Tournament

Ventura, anchored to the baseline, looked totally bewildered as he failed to acclimatise to the very different conditions offered by grass courts and was given a 6-1 6-2 drubbing by the ruthless Scot, who completed his first ATP tour win in fine style. Murray said afterwards: 'I didn't find the transition that tough but it was obviously a big match for me and the first win is always an important one. When I played my first main tournament in Barcelona I lost a tough match and felt bad afterwards but this time I knew what the other guy was going to play like and it obviously wasn't his best surface. It wasn't as tough as some other matches are going to be on grass.'

True enough, the second round offered a greater examination of Murray's grass-court credentials as it threw up the imposing figure of big-serving Taylor Dent, seeded ninth for the tournament. However, as the Scot was rapidly showing, the bigger the occasion the greater he plays, as he overpowered Dent comfortably, winning 6-3 6-3.

The assured manner in which he achieved two timely breaks in the first set and one in the second were more redolent of a seasoned pro than an inexperienced youth. Murray was rightly delighted with himself, commenting: 'I played great today and I'm so pleased with myself. I felt going in I had a chance because I return so well and I managed to get onto his serve in the first few games. I dealt with it well and I didn't really have any nerves for my first time in front of a big home crowd.'

Accompanying Murray in his quest to become king at Queen's was head of men's training at the Lawn Tennis Association, Mark Petchey, who had offered to help steer the teenager through the grass-court season. At last Murray was back in the hands of an experienced coach. Everything was coming together nicely. Petchey himself was excited at the prospect of working with Murray, declaring after the Dent game: 'A few of the shots he produced in that match some of us can only dream of.'

Eager to avoid any undue hype, Petchey added of

Murray: 'Potentially he could be a great player, but everybody needs to be realistic about where they see him in six months or a year. We don't need to rush it. There are a lot of expectations on his shoulders. When we see somebody like him everybody wants him to be the next Tim Henman. That is difficult because Tim has been phenomenally consistent in his career and achieved more than people give him credit for. But in Andy's mind there is no Plan B. Tennis is his life and he is going to make the most of it. What I would like our other young players to take from him is the heart and desire he shows on court. He has an

Murray reaches the third round at Queen's Club and takes on former Australian Open champion Thomas Johansson. In a pulsating game, the pair swap sets before, at 3-3 in the third, disaster strikes for the ill-fated teenager when he falls and injures his ankle...

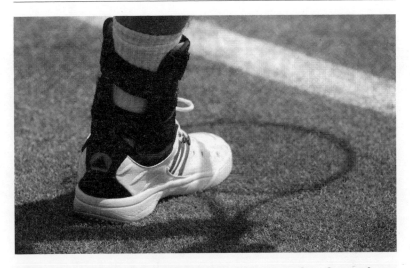

...but he recovers in time for the tennis showpiece event of the summer.

unquenchable thirst to compete and that will stand him in good stead.'

Thomas Johansson, 2002 Australian Open champion, now stood between Murray and a possible dream meeting with Tim Henman.

The third-round match was an intensely competitive, close affair which always looked likely to be decided by narrow margins. Johansson edged the first set, winning a tie break 7-1, before Murray hit back to win the second set 7-6. The events of the deciding set were to be a defining moment in Murray's year as, with the match finely poised at 3-3, cramp set in to cruelly halt the teenager's momentum. His worsening condition led to an agonising fall on the baseline, causing Murray to injure his ankle. Although Murray resumed play following lengthy treatment, he could barely walk, let alone run, and Johansson took the set and match, 7-5.

It was a sad end to what had been an enjoyable snapshot of Murray's capabilities, although the British public had seen enough to be assured that Tim Henman's successor had arrived.

The young Scot was, however, inconsolable in defeat. 'I thought I was going to win when I was 30-0 up at 5-4 in the third set,' he admitted. 'When I went over on the ankle, I could have got up but I thought I heard something crack so didn't want to take any risks.' Meanwhile, Thomas Johansson offered a glowing endorsement of both Murray's performance and his future prospects. He told reporters: 'I'm very impressed with the way he's playing – especially his serve and his ground strokes – and he's going to get even better.'

'HE'S ONE OF THOSE GUYS THAT, TO ME, WAS BORN TO BE A TENNIS PLAYER.'

John McEnroe on Andrew Murray

His ankle injured, it looked as though Murray would miss Wimbledon. But an MRI scan revealed that no bones were broken and he was passed fit to play, so long as he missed the Nottingham Open to allow the inflammation to die down. Yet while Andrew's inflamed ankle calmed down, an inflamed public flared up into a mini-outbreak of Murray Mania. A Who's Who of tennis legends was lined up by the media to offer their newly-minted opinions of the Scot. Boris Becker called him 'a fresh and exciting' talent, capable of becoming the figurehead of British men's tennis for years to come. John McEnroe, never short of an opinion, also poked his greying head above the parapet to eulogise the teenage star. He also revealed that he had offered to coach Murray on a part-time basis – and that he was genuinely upset that neither camp had been able to make it happen. He revealed: 'This has been talked about a little bit and for whatever reason it just hasn't happened. Andy is a talent and for whatever reason, the people at the LTA or whoever, it hasn't happened. It's somewhat disappointing.' He then added: 'I'd like to work with him but I'm not going to travel the circuit with him. His talent's there and he is headed in the right direction. He's one of those guys that, to me, was born to be a tennis player. Now he's got to take advantage of that talent.'

When McEnroe speaks, you must sit up and listen. Although it seemed unlikely that he would ever be involved in coaching Murray on a permanent basis, he would do the next best thing by endorsing his every move through the professional ranks. This, if nothing else, is testament to the irrepressible Scot's character and resolve that he had managed to turn his chief destroyer from the Superset event into his principal supporter within less than a year.

Before long, Andrew Murray would be winning over many more supporters.

CHAPTER 6

THE WONDER OF WIMBLEDON

ASK ANY aspiring British tennis player which tournament they covet the most and as sure as strawberries go with cream the response is certain to be: 'Wimbledon'. True to form, Andrew Murray is the exception to the rule. To him Wimbledon represents much that is wrong with tennis. Its stuffiness, its exclusiveness and its hide-bound, rule-bound general air of uptightness were all anathema to the freewheeling teenager.

Before Wimbledon 2005 he told *The Sunday Times:* 'At Wimbledon the all-white clothing rule may be fine for 50-year-olds watching, but it hardly appeals to people my age. They want to see players running around in the latest outfits and looking sharp, not stuck in the dark ages. That's why [tennis] isn't as popular in Britain as it is in other countries. Young people just think it's boring.'

As well as its restrictive dress code, there was a more personal reason why Murray was not enamoured of the blazered guardians of British tennis at Wimbledon's All England Club: he claims officials at the All England Club refused to enter into a reciprocal agreement with their US Open counterparts to allow the Scot a wildcard at the American Grand Slam.

It is understood that organisers of the US Open would have handed Murray a wildcard had those in charge at Wimbledon guaranteed an American a similar prize; the alleged refusal to promote transatlantic relations by the British left the Scot feeling aggrieved, believing his efforts at SW19 deserved better treatment.

In any case, Murray freely admits that the US Open is his favourite Grand Slam tournament for its more relaxed approach to how players should behave and dress themselves. He is also a self-proclaimed admirer of the raucous razzmatazz generated at Flushing Meadows and the reverential way players are treated in America. The basic facilities on offer at Wimbledon, combined with the often buttoned-up restraint of the show court crowds, was less to Murray's liking, too.

Furthermore, Murray's indifference to the lush lawns of SW19 can also be attributed to the fact that his upbringing in Spain had left him with a fondness for clay or hard courts over grass.

Yet, like it or not, Wimbledon is still the Big One, the tournament by which all champions are measured. Even grass court non-naturals, such as Björn Borg and Andre Agassi, had overcome their limitations on the surface to become tournament legends. Talent and perseverance had been the keys to their success on the surface – two qualities that Murray possessed in abundance.

However, repeating Borg and Agassi's triumphs at Wimbledon are some way off for Murray, in the (hopefully) not-too-distant future. Taking on the mantle of the Great New British Hope, he battled his way through the first and second rounds – disposing of Switzerland's George Bastl and Radek Stepanek of the Czech Republic on the way – before earning a third-round appearance on Centre Court against the Argentinian powerhouse David Nalbandian. Murray gave his all against his stronger, older opponent, winning the first two sets, but eventually lost in five nerve-shredding sets as cramp and fatigue set in. He was understandably upset, but the crowd loved it. They had a new hero.

Such an emotional roller-coaster ride was a far cry from Murray's inauspicious Wimbledon debut in 2002, when, aged just 15, he was the youngest entrant that year in the juniors' competition. Not only did he exit in the first round of the singles, losing 7-6 4-6 6-4 to Belarus's Alexander Skrypko, he did not fare much better in the doubles – he and fellow Scot David Brewer succumbed 6-4, 6-4 in the second round to German pairing Markus Bayer and Philipp Petzschner, the number one seeds.

It is interesting to note that at this juncture 17-year-old Brewer was considered more of a prospect than Murray. He recalls how his younger playing partner would quiz him on how to work his way up the rankings: 'He was asking: "How many points do I get for this?", I'm like: "30", and he's like: "How many have you got?" I say "300", and he says: "Oh, I'm never going to get there." But it's just gradual build-up; I tell him: "You'll get points every week if you keep performing," and he's like "Oh, okay".' Three years later, while Murray became a household name and had surged into the Top 70 best players in the world, Brewer had yet to consolidate his youthful promise, being ranked 1,266 in December 2005.

Meanwhile, back in 2003, Murray continued to find the adjustment from clay to grass a testing experience. He revealed: 'It takes time to get used to the different surface, although I'm much quicker on grass now than I was before. But going from clay to grass is quite a change. The bounce is completely different for a start – the ball bounces lower – the points are much faster and it's more tiring on the legs, as you have to bend them more because of the low bounce.'

Frustratingly for the Scot, his grass-court woes continued when he failed to justify his tenth seeding for the juniors' tournament and again tumbled out at the first round, losing 6-4, 6-4 to German Peter Steinberger. The doubles proved more fertile territory for the young Murray, however, as he and partner Tom Rushby reached the semi-finals, where they were overpowered by defending champions Florin Mergea and Horia Tecau 6-3 7-5.

By 2004, the Scot was determined that he would finally blossom on the lush green, green grass of home and, given the fact he was then rated as the world's second best junior behind France's Gaël Monfils, was confident of reversing his recent trend of struggling to translate his fine worldwide performances on to the Wimbledon stage. He won his way through to the third round, where he was defeated 7-5 6-3 by the Korean, Woong-Sun Jun. It wasn't the progress Murray quite had in mind, but it was better than anything he had achieved at Wimbledon before.

A year later, Murray had left the juniors behind and was ready to pit his wits against the best of the best.

As a mark of his progress, together with fellow British males Josh Goodall, Alan Mackin, Jonathan Marray and David Sherwood, Andrew Murray was given a wildcard for Wimbledon 2005.

His first opponent was a young Swiss who had earned a place in history with a stunning upset at Wimbledon in 2002. No, this wasn't Roger Federer but George Bastl, who had stunned the tennis world that year when he ended seven-times winner Pete Sampras's Wimbledon career by sensationally knocking the legend out of the tournament in the second round.

But Bastl's career had failed to progress since that fateful day and he looked eminently beatable on paper. Murray could draw further confidence from the fact that his Swiss opponent had only played one match on grass that year prior to Wimbledon – losing in the first round of the Surbiton Challenger. On the minus side, it remained to be seen if the ankle injury that Murray had sustained at the Stella Artois tournament just weeks before Wimbledon had healed sufficiently.

Judy Murray was cautiously optimistic, and told the BBC: 'I reckon he can win his first round. What will be tough for him is that he would have lost a bit of fitness after having twisted his ankle. But if he plays well then he will have a chance.'

For most 18-year-olds, the tremendous weight of

expectation and nervous anticipation of a Wimbledon debut would be too much to bear, but from the minute Andrew Murray strode nonchalantly onto Court Number Two, it was apparent that this was no ordinary teenager. With his straggly, curly hair just about held in check by a baseball cap, a pair of headphone wires could just be detected running down to an iPod. As he loped onto the field of play, Murray was listening to the Black Eyed Peas' 'Let's Get It Started', a shout-out, feel-good track that Murray listened to to get him in the mood for a big match.

100 minutes after play started Murray was jogging to the net to congratulate his defeated opponent. Murray had swept Bastl aside 6-4 6-2 6-2 in a comfortable display punctuated by a flurry of whoops, fist-clenches and motivational 'Come ons', all against the cacophonous backdrop of an increasingly uproarious home crowd.

In what could be seen as an era-defining moment, the so-called 'Henman Hill' outside the main courts, where tennis fans gathered to watch the action on a big screen, was quickly re-dubbed 'Murray Field' – if only for the day. Even at this early stage Murray, with is youth and enthusiasm, seemed to have captured the public's imagination.

Murray's Scottishness was emphatically made clear when he publicly corrected Bud Collins, a reporter for the *Boston Globe*, for mistakenly calling him English in the after-match press conference. 'No one in the States imagined an English kid could win the US Junior Open,' said a geographically-confused Collins, before being tersely informed of his error by Murray.

Murray's next opponent was Radek Stepanek, an unpredictable yet gifted Czech ranked 13 in the world. John McEnroe warned that: 'Radek Stepanek is a guy who is very difficult to read. Even if Murray's mum goes out and video-cams his first-round match and studies him, she's going to find out that even Stepanek doesn't know where he's going to hit the ball sometimes.' Radek Stepanek would, in theory, offer a rigorous examination of Murray's grass-court credentials, especially as the game would be played on Court Number One, a daunting, atmosphere-filled arena for even the most experienced player.

In the event, Stepanek could not cope with Murray's magnificent onslaught as the Scot displayed a dazzling repertoire of cultured lobs, heavily sliced backhands and classy top-spin forehands to cap a stylish 6-4 6-4 6-4 victory. Murray made a mockery of his world ranking of 312 by toying with his outclassed opponent. He even withstood a desperate act of gamesmanship by Stepanek towards the end of the match.

'I WAS A LITTLE BIT DISAPPOINTED WITH HIM AT THE END BECAUSE HE WAS TRYING TO PUT ME OFF.'

Andrew Murray criticises Radek Stepanek's gamesmanship after their 2005 Wimbledon match

With the tie slipping away from him, Stepanek began to glare menacingly at Murray after each point the Scot lost, in an effort to psyche him out. Murray revealed: 'I was a little bit disappointed with him at the end because he was trying to put me off. Everybody told me before the match that he was going to try a bit of gamesmanship and ends up looking a bit stupid because he lost.'

Despite suffering from a sore head and stomach due to eating a 'dodgy' curry the night before, Murray had worked the 11,500 crowd into a frenzy with his animated facial expressions, boundless enthusiasm and unquenchable desire to win. 'If he keeps pumping his fist like that, within a year he'll have a forearm like Rafael Nadal,' said Boris Becker, a man who knows a thing or two about exuberant celebrations.

Murray's victory stood in stark contrast to Tim Henman's defeat at the hands of Russia's Dimitri Tursunov in the same round, where he exited the tournament in foul-mouthed fashion after clashing with both the umpire and the crowd. Writing in the

Daily Telegraph, sports journalist Jim White pointed out that Henman was a strangely passionless performer, whereas Murray's emotions were out there for all to see: 'Murray exudes an attitude that is almost Australian. He has a huge mouth, which forms itself into a rectangular roar of triumph or yelp of rage at the end of virtually every shot. He snorts and snarls, and when he clenches his hands in celebration of a point, he really looks as though he means it.'

Characteristically, Murray embellished his energetic and inspirational display against Stepanek with a celebratory yelp of delight and a hop, skip and jump up to the net, while his proud mother Judy wept and clapped in the stands alongside his brother Jamie and coach Mark Petchey.

It was sheer epiphany – a defining moment in Murray's career to date.

Suddenly everyone was clamouring for a piece of the Scottish star – including awestruck females in the crowd, who held up a banner advertising their availability for marriage. Ignoring the microphones thrust in his

> **'Murray exudes an attitude that is almost Australian... He snorts and snarls, and when he clenches his hands in celebration of a point, he really looks as though he means it.'**
>
> Jim White of the
> *Daily Telegraph*

Murray's grandparents, Roy and Shirley Erskine, are captivated by their grandson's Wimbledon exploits.

direction, Murray instead spent time signing autographs – honouring his promise to never refuse to sign his name for a fan if possible.

Then, in a wonderful piece of tennis theatre, Murray turned to the waiting BBC reporter, Gary Richardson, a terrier-like interviewer famed for getting under the skin of his interviewees and prompting them to reveal more than they actually wanted to say. 'How on earth have you just beaten a man ranked 13 in the world when you are 312th?', Richardson probed. Murray's response was tantalisingly terse: 'By playing well.' Game, set and match to Murray!

But while Andrew way playing it cool, the rest of the Murray clan was revelling in the young maestro's triumph – although it was a slightly bittersweet moment for his Roy Erskine: he had bet £10 on his grandson losing!

The odds looked heavily stacked against a Murray win in the third round. He was drawn against the former Wimbledon finalist David Nalbandian of Argentina, the 18th seed. Murray offered an honest assessment of what he was up

Talented Czech Radek Stepanek rests but in the end he proved no match for Andy in the second round at Wimbledon 2005.

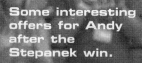
Some interesting
offers for Andy
after the
Stepanek win.

Will You
arry Me Andy?

against. 'I'll lose my next match. Nalbandian is top 10 in the world, he's been to a Wimbledon final,' he said.

Nevertheless, Murray was able to approach the match brimming with confidence. He already had two great wins under his belt, plus the Wimbledon crowd was firmly on his side. Nalbandian was also known to be suspect when the pressure was really on. And as the match was to be played on Centre Court, one of the most pressure-inducing arenas in the world, the stage was surely set for anything to happen.

The stars came out for Murray's match against Nalbandian. Sir Steven Redgrave, Sir Matthew Pinsent, Sir Sean Connery, Lawrence Dallaglio, John Terry, Jayne Torvill and many more squeezed into the Royal Box to see of Andrew could pull it off. The signs looked promising as he loped onto Centre Court, head bobbing rhythmically to the Black Eyed Peas blasting through his iPod, with seemingly not a care in the world. The 13,000 crowd went wild, but Murray was oblivious, lost in his own world of music.

Swept along by the crowd and the intensity of the occasion, Murray blitzed Nalbandian, winning the first two sets 7-6 6-1. It was a storming display from the great Scot, full of passion, prowess and panache that left his appreciably more experienced

Former James Bond star Sir Sean Connery later said Andy gave one of the finest exhibitions of tennis he had seen at Wimbledon.

opponent bewildered, forcing him into a rash of unforced errors.

Then, it all began to go wrong. Tennis a game of very fine margins, and the smallest factors can turn matches. Despite his two-set lead, Murray's old fitness problems suddenly returned to haunt him. He began to cramp up and Nalbandian, sensing that this was his only opportunity to salvage something, took full advantage. As Murray's fitness deteriorated, Nalbandian pulled himself together and took the third set 6-0. The atmosphere in Centre Court and out on Murray Field changed dramatically. Here we go again.

Apart from the occasional plaintive cry of 'Come on Andy!' from the crowd, a deathly hush settled over the spectators. Tiring and in pain, Murray resorted to easing up and conserving his strength, with the aim of re-energising himself for a concerted effort to take the fourth set. But by this time, the Argentine's class, superior conditioning and experience were beginning to prove decisive. Much to Murray's dismay the 2002 Wimbledon men's beaten finalist prevailed 6-4.

Hobbling, scowling and cursing, reverting to type as an 'It's-all-so-unfair' teenager, Murray succumbed to the inevitable and surrendered the final set 6-1.

Murray and his ardent fans were naturally disappointed that his exhilarating Wimbledon journey had ended in the cul-de-sac of bitter defeat, but there was also a realisation that, had it not been for his physical limitations, Andrew could well have vanquished the experienced Nalbandian. It should be remembered that this was the first five-set match that Andrew Murray had ever played in a senior tournament – and a Grand Slam tournament at that.

The cumulative effect of nerves, tension and intense competition following a period on the sidelines had taken its toll, yet Murray emerged with immense credit for a scintillating early summer which had seen him blaze a trail up the rankings – he had rocketed 99 places to 213 in the world.

'WHEN I GOT BACK IN THE LOCKER ROOM, MY LEGS WERE SO TIRED I COULDN'T GET UP. I JUST GOT TIRED BECAUSE I'VE NEVER PLAYED A FIVE-SET MATCH BEFORE.'

Murray after defeat by David Nalbandian at
Wimbledon 2005

Murray later admitted: 'I was annoyed I couldn't keep going in the fifth set. I felt I was running around OK in the fourth, but in the fifth, I really started to feel tired. When I got back in the locker room, my legs were so tired I couldn't get up. I just got tired because I've never played a five-set match before.' Murray was determined not to be too gloomy, though, adding: 'I wasn't expecting to do so well so I have to look at it positively. In a few days I'm sure I'll realise what I've done and I'll be proud of myself.'

The Scot was determined he would sample more occasions like his Centre Court debut, adding: 'The support when I walked off Centre Court made me feel like I belonged there. I want to play in big tournaments and I have proved to myself that I can.'

David Nalbandian confirmed after the match that he believed Murray had lost because of his physical conditioning. In effect, he was saying that he had not won the match, but that Murray had lost it.

Up in the Royal Box, Sir Sean Connery, again commenting on Murray's apparent lack of preparation and fitness, offered this blunt assessment of what Murray needed in order to succeed: 'Somebody has to get their s**t off the ground and help Murray, appoint Mark Petchey, with whatever Petchey recommends. He beat Radek Stepanek, who had three coaches and was seeded, and Murray, who had one, beat him. You tell me we have a problem, I can solve it in two minutes.'

Interestingly, while Murray appreciated Connery's words of advice and encouragement – Sir Sean sent him a 'good luck' text message prior to the match – Murray admitted he was more touched Tim Henman's praise of his achievements after the game.

> **'The support when I walked off Centre Court made me feel like I belonged there. I want to play in big tournaments and I have proved to myself that I can,'**
>
> Andrew Murray at Wimbledon, 2005

While SW19 buzzed and bubbled with Murray's thrill-a-minute, roller-coaster exploits, back in Dunblane the locals were even more excited by Andrew's progress. Before the Nalbandian match, the town's few betting shops were doing a roaring trade in wagers on Murray to beat the Argentine. High street shops proudly displayed posters of their former townsman and

Murray's favourite Indian restaurant, the India Gate, had even created a curry in his honour.

Amid all the hysteria, Jimmy Connors struck exactly the correct tone when he described the aftermath of Murray's loss as 'day one of the rest of his career'.

'LIFE AS HE KNEW IT WILL NEVER BE QUITE THE SAME AGAIN FOR ANDY MURRAY; WHILE THE ENTIRE NATION HAS SADLY REACHED THE CONCLUSION THAT TIM HENMAN WILL NOT NOW FULFIL OUR YEARNINGS BY WINNING WIMBLEDON, SO THE 18-YEAR-OLD SCOT HAS BECAME THE "ANOINTED ONE" IN HIS STEAD,'

The Daily Telegraph after Andrew Murray's first Wimbledon

Andrew's debut at Wimbledon marked the official start of 'Murray Mania'. According to *The Daily Telegraph*: 'Life as he knew it will never be quite the same again for Andy Murray; while the entire nation has sadly reached the conclusion that Tim Henman will not now fulfil our yearnings by winning Wimbledon, so the 18-year-old Scot has became the "anointed one" in his stead.'

Sensibly, though perhaps unrealistically, Murray implored those hailing him as Britain's new tennis saviour to lower their expectations of him, especially in regard to his winning Wimbledon. Murray's plea for a little realism was backed by American tennis guru Nick Bollettieri, who had overseen the development of Andre Agassi and Maria Sharapova. According to Bollettieri, Murray: 'Has only had one bit of success and, although he could be something, he is nothing yet. It is important that his energy is channelled in the

Andy and Israeli Shahar Peer partnered in the Wimbledon mixed doubles in 2005.

right direction but it is nice to see the spirit and confidence he has. He's a very confident young man who shows his emotions and there is nothing wrong with that.'

Defeat at the hands of David Nalbandian did not mark the end of Murray's Wimbledon that year. He was also entered in the mixed doubles, where he partnered the 18-year-old Israeli, Shahar Peer. Their appearance on Court No. 3 was greeted by the sort of cheers usually reserved for Centre Court finalists. Unfortunately it was very much a case of 'after the Lord Mayor's show', as Murray and Peer's confrontation with Lucas Arnold of Argentina and Emanuelle Gagliardi of Switzerland was a distinct anti-climax.

'I'm sorry if any young girls are jealous of me. If they want to swap places they can always call me.'

Shahar Peer,
Andrew Murray's
mixed doubles
partner at
Wimbledon 2005

Murray could understandably not summon up the same stunning levels of intensity and dizzying momentum as he had generated before a television audience of 9.3 million against Nalbandian. He and his partner were defeated 3-6, 4-6. With typically harsh self-assessment, Murray took all the blame on himself: '[Peer] played much better than me. I was rubbish. I've never played mixed doubles before so

I didn't know what to do and was scared of hitting it to the girl.'

Peer, who along with Murray, became part of the first doubles pair to attend a press conference in the main media room, added charmingly of her desire to play with the sought-after Scot: 'I wrote him an e-mail during the French Open because I wanted to play mixed doubles at Wimbledon and I thought he would get a wildcard and I wouldn't. I've known him since we were about 12 so I thought, "Why not try it?" I'm sorry if any young girls are jealous of me. If they want to swap places they can always call me.'

'I'M SUPPOSED TO BE SEEING COLDPLAY TONIGHT, SO I WANT TO BE OUT OF WIMBLEDON!'

Murray on the eve of his 2005 Wimbledon doubles defeat

However, one of Murray's comments before his doubles match did come back to bite him. Asked what his plans were for the week, Murray replied: 'I'm supposed to be seeing Coldplay tonight, so I want to be out of Wimbledon!' When he and Peer duly lost their match that day he was inevitably accused of taking his tennis less than seriously.

While his final appearance at Wimbledon 2005 may have been underwhelming, few now doubted that Murray would one day become a major player there. The only question is: When? In February 2006 Andrew Murray replaced Tim Henman as the British number one, so from now on he will have to carry that extra burden of weight and responsibility around with him.

Will 2006 be Andrew Murray's year? Bookmakers William Hill have already slashed the odds on his winning Wimbledon 2006 from 25/1 to 16/1, showing an admirable cautious optimism. As for Murray himself, only time will tell...

CHAPTER 7

RULE BRITANNIA

WHAT IS it about the British and tennis? For two weeks of the year, Wimbledon fortnight, Britons are the most passionate tennis fans in the world; everyone becomes an instant expert on the sport and all eyes are turned to SW19. Yet as soon as the tournament ends the nation sinks into a kind of collective amnesia and forgets all about tennis for another year.

The reason for this is very simple: Britain simply isn't very good at tennis. With the notable exceptions of Tim Henman and Greg Rusedski – neither of whom has ever truly made it to the very top – Britain has few players of note. Add to this the dearth of major tennis events held in the UK and the country's 50-week indifference to the sport becomes understandable.

Can Andrew Murray buck this dismal trend,

banish British apathy and reinvigorate a success-starved nation's interest in tennis? As with many factors regarding Andrew Murray, it's too soon to tell – but the signs are more positive than they have been for any other player for years.

Age is the first factor on Murray's side. He's still only a very young man and has plenty of years of tennis in him. In fact, the main thing he needs to concentrate on at this stage in his career is making sure that his body is 'right'. As he continues to grow and develop, Andrew and his advisors must ensure that he does not over-extend himself on what is a punishing world tour of tennis events. He no longer seems to suffer as much from the paralysing cramps that regularly used to afflict him, so the indicators are that his conditioning is coming together nicely.

Then there is the issue of motivation; would Murray be able to summon up the same levels of drive and enthusiasm as he had demonstrated during high-profile, adrenaline-inducing matches in his homeland? How would he react when playing in front of sparse crowds at some obscure tournament in Eastern Europe? Or, more importantly, when facing a hostile mob as he played against a local favourite? Given Murray's volatile temper, it was something that needed to be asked.

These frequently-asked questions were answered

with an emphatic 'Yes' as Murray made a meteoric rise up the rankings. Not only would his thrilling ascent bring financial reward from the tournaments he entered, but the savvy Scot ensured his pockets would be lined after betting that he would be the first of Britain's crop of emerging young players to reach the Top 100 in the world.

> **'I find it difficult to get pumped up to play in the smaller tournaments.'**
>
> Andrew Murray
> on motivation

After Wimbledon, Murray, Davis Cup doubles partner David Sherwood and fellow team-mates Alex Bogdanovic and Greg Rusedski wagered £100 each on which of the British babes would be the first to join the Canadian-born Brit in the Top 100. Murray explained: 'If I am first I will get £300, but the best thing will be taking the money off the other guys! I would like to reach the Top 100 before the end of this year. That was my goal and it's still my goal.'

Addressing the motivation issue in early 2006 issue he admitted, 'It's much different playing in front of a crowd like [Wimbledon] than going and playing some of the tournaments that I've been playing when there's maybe five or six people watching. It's very difficult. I find it difficult to get pumped up to play in the smaller tournaments so I probably won't play any more junior events now.

Hero in waiting: Andy Murray even younger than when he first started making international waves – but not by that much.

Andy fooling around for the cameras.

Andy with his mother Judy Murray.

Top: Murray and his coach Mark Petchey in discussion at the start of 2006.

Below: With the British Davis Cup team in September, 2005.

Excellent training in Spain helped Andy develop his skill and power.

Top: Murray makes his senior men's debut at Wimbledon and defeats George Bastl in straight sets in the first round.

Bottom: The disconsolate Scot contemplates defeat to David Nalbandian in a five-set thriller in the third round of Wimbledon 2005.

Top: Every emotion, joy or pain, is evident on Andy's face throughout his matches.

Below left: Forget Henmania – now it's Murraymania.

Below right: Andy signs autographs at the US Open in 2005.

Top: Shhh! One finger to those in the media questioning his fitness after seeing off Pavel in stifling heat at Flushing Meadows.

Below: Andy relaxes at home.

I'm looking at moving my ranking up to the Top 100 by the end of the year so it's best to spend my time playing in the senior events and hopefully what I've done here will give me the chance to get some more wildcards into some of the bigger men's events, and that would help me reach my goal more quickly.'

Thankfully for the Scot, his first tournament after Wimbledon would be in a country whose warmth, exuberance and competitive spirit matches his own – the USA.

Murray began his ambitious personal quest to infiltrate the Top 100 at the Hall of Fame Championships in Rhode Island. Looking at the draw, Murray saw that if he made it through to the quarter-finals he would potentially face the British number two, Greg Rusedski. Frenchman Gregory Carraz, world-ranked 126, was the first obstacle in the way of this mouth-watering prospect. Consequently, he was comfortably disposed of 6-4 7-5 by his lower-ranked opponent. Murray hailed the victory as 'one of the biggest of my life'.

Next up was another Frenchman, the world 111 Antony Dupuis. Here desire came up against harsh reality as the rankings book came crashing down on Murray with a loud thud. Dupuis easily overcame Murray in a 6-4 6-1 win. Murray blamed the Newport grass courts, where the balls had a tendency to stay low, for this unwelcome reality check.

Things went much better in Murray's next tournament, a Challenger event in Aptos, California, where he had been awarded a wildcard. He eased past Canadian Frederic Niemeyer 6-2 6-4 in the first round, before his expected second-round opponent Justin Gimelstob withdrew to injury. The Australian, Marc Kimmich, a 'lucky loser' entrant to the event, was brushed aside 6-4 7-5, handing Murray a game against experienced Israeli, Harel Levy.

The veteran campaigner had represented his country against Great Britain, losing one and winning the other of his singles match in the Davis Cup tie several months earlier, but could not add another British scalp to his name as the Scot won with consummate ease, 6-4 6-0. A 6-3 6-4 triumph over American Bobby Reynolds in the semi-finals put Murray in with a great chance of his first Challenger trophy, and afforded him a golden opportunity to make a major leap up the world rankings.

The opportunistic youngster gratefully seized both openings and won out 6-4 6-3 over American Rajeev Ram, shooting up 41 ranking places to 164. In securing his win, Murray became the youngest winner of the event in its 19-year history. He also picked up a useful £6,150 in pocket money. All in all, not a bad day's work. 'It was a big win for me and has given me a lot of confidence,' was Murray's token response to his landmark success.

After this, there was to be no respite for the itinerant Scot. Crossing the vast continent, he touched down in Indianapolis for the RCA Championships. Despite suffering from tiredness after his long journey from California, Murray still proved too strong for his first-round opponent, Jess Witten, winning 6-4 6-2.

Again, the reality of life on the Tour – and the fact that the world rankings are there for a reason – got the better of Murray in the next round. Mardy Fish, the 2004 Olympic silver medallist and world ranked at 16, overpowered Andrew in three hard-fought sets, 6-4 4-6 6-4. At one point, Murray had even led 3-1 in the final set.

Another day, another tournament. Touching down in Canada, Murray next took part in the Granby Challenger event. He came out on top in the battle of the Brits, beating Richard Bloomfield 6-2 7-6 in the first round, before clinching a quarter-final place with a 6-3 7-5 success over Romania's Florin Mergea. Unfortunately, his hopes of success were dashed by Frenchman Gregory Carraz, who won 6-3 7-6.

Murray also progressed to the quarter-final stage of the Vancouver Open with wins over Marc Kimmich and Cecil Mamiit, before falling to

Australia's Paul Baccanello. He was now edging ever closer to his ambition of entering the world Top 100, having risen to 145 in the ATP rankings through an impressive accumulation of points.

The dBI Challenger tournament in Binghamton, New York, represented Murray's next test and one which he commenced in style with a resounding 6-3 6-1 over Harel Levy. However, the untimely intervention of the weather – play was postponed due to rain – meant that the young Scot was then faced with the unenviable prospect of two matches in a day to reach the final.

The tight scheduling made little difference to an unruffled Murray, though, as he first accounted for Alex Bogomolov, 6-4 6-4, and then ran out a comfortable 6-2 6-3 winner against fifth seed Brian Baker in the semi-finals. In the final, he reeled off his third match win in two days by seeing off the challenge of Colombian Alejandro Falla, 7-6 6-3, to clinch his second Challenger crown within a month.

The satisfied Scot said: 'Alejandro has gone through qualifying and so he's played a lot of matches and he started out very well. I managed to hold serve pretty well today and I played a pretty solid match.' The result had imbued him with confidence that he could, in the not too distant future, break into the world's Top 100. He added: 'I think I'm ready, maybe physically I'm not in as good shape as a lot of the guys inside the Top 100 – but I think my tennis is there. This isn't the same as winning on the ATP tour, but winning these tournaments gives you a lot of confidence because there are still a lot of good players here.'

It was now time for Murray to move away from the world of journeymen and youthful talents like himself and enter the arena of established stars for his first ATP Masters series event in Cincinnati.

Once again he excelled when faced with a higher-ranked player. He more than held his own against the thunderous serving of American Taylor Dent, squeaking through on two tie-breaks, 7-4 and 7-1. The Scot pronounced himself pleased with the composure and solidity of his performance, adding that he was pleased to be operating away from the stifling, pressure-filled environment of Britain.

The imposing figure of the mercurial Russian Marat Safin stood before Murray and further progress in what arguably represented the Dunblane man's most demanding match in his professional career. After losing the first set 6-4, Murray took advantage of some alarming, but not totally out-of-character,unforced errors from the 1m 93cm (6ft 4in) Safin to stunningly seal the second set 6-1.

However, the enigmatic Safin regained his composure and began to unleash winner after winner. A 6-1 third set drubbing completed Safin's win and Murray's exit, although this was hardly a disgrace following a creditable showing against one of the best players in the world.

'UNTIL YOU START BEATING SOME OF THE BEST PLAYERS, YOU DON'T GET THE RESPECT OF THE TOP GUYS,'

Andy Murray

Sadly, Murray's laudable efforts had not persuaded US Open officials to hand him a wild card for their forthcoming New York showpiece. A crestfallen Murray admitted: 'I think it takes a while to get the respect because, obviously, I'm still not inside the Top 100. Until you start beating some of the best players, you don't get the respect of the top guys.' Stuck on a never-ending conveyor belt of challenges, Murray would now have to win three more matches to secure qualification for Flushing Meadows.

The first of those three victories was achieved against Israel's Dudi Sela, with a routine 6-4 6-4 win. He then put the Italian Paolo Lorenzi to the sword, 6-3 6-2, in the first qualifying round. Finally, he vanquished Ecuador's Giovanni Lapentii 6-0 7-6 to secure a place in the US Open as a senior – just one year after he had claimed the junior crown.

According to the defiant youngster, his displays

since Wimbledon and the subsequent garnering of two trophies was irrefutable evidence that he had the staying power and ability to cope with the incessant pressures of top-level tennis. He asserted: 'Every single person in Britain is so negative about the young players. All they are waiting to do is just put them down, and I think this week I have showed that possibly I might go on and do well.'

> **'Every single person in Britain is so negative about the young players. All they are waiting to do is just put them down.'**
>
> Andrew Murray lashes out at his countrymen

Murray arrived at Flushing Meadows in less than tip-top shape, still nursing an injured shoulder sustained during his defeat to Safin. However, this was offset by his mental condition, which was razor sharp. He was still buzzing from his performances during the summer that had filled him with confidence.

He was also relishing taking part in his first seniors' US Open, which he rates as his favourite tournament. The carnival atmosphere, the noise, music and vibrant colour that prevails at Flushing Meadows suited the impressionable teenager down to the ground. The US Open is almost like an amusement park, with a tennis tournament attached. What young person can resist that?

Murray cries out in delight at the US Open in 2005.

'THE NIGHT MATCHES ARE COOL; THE ATMOSPHERE IS GREAT. I LIKE TO PLAY IN NEW YORK AS THE FANS ARE REALLY NOISY AND THEY SUPPORT THE GUY WHO IS BEHIND AS THEY WANT TO SEE GOOD, CLOSE TENNIS.'

Andrew Murray on the US Open

Murray gushed: 'They play music during the change of ends and there's lots of noise and excitement. It's a got a real buzz about it, it's more rock'n'roll, so it attracts a much younger audience as well as traditional tennis fans. The night matches are cool; the atmosphere is great. I like to

Andy surges into a two-set lead against Arnaud Clement of France in the second round of the US Open in 2005. But it proves impossible to maintain his lead.

play in New York as the fans are really noisy and they support the guy who is behind as they want to see good, close tennis.'

Murray's admiration for all things American was reciprocated. The American fans had grown to love him, as had many of the pundits who admired his freewheeling, blood-and-guts approach. In their eyes, Murray was up there with Rafael Nadal, the buccaneering Spaniard who looks – and plays – like a marauding pirate.

Murray's place in the hearts of his American audience was sealed by his first round victory over world number 39 Andrei Pavel in five gruelling sets of tennis, which ran out at 6-3 3-6 3-6 6-1 6-4. Andrew gave his all in this match, and at one point he astonished the crowd by vomiting on court

Throwing in the towel – defeat in New York.

Murray and Clement shake hands after their five-set battle.

during the final set, delaying proceedings for 21 minutes. The spectators seemed to be fascinated by Murray's sickness. It recalled Pete Sampras's astonishing evacuation of bodily fluids during his 1996 quarter-final with Alex Corretja, which he won on the way to eventual US Open glory. If it was good enough for Pistol Pete, why not for Murray, too?

'I THOUGHT IT WAS PRETTY FUNNY. I THOUGHT THAT I WAS GOING TO BURP AND SUDDENLY I THREW UP,'

Andrew Murray on vomiting on court during the US Open

Afterwards, a laconic Murray preferred to play down his violent and graphic illness. He blamed it on a sodium-rich energy drink that he had gulped down eagerly in a bid to stave off the onset of cramp. He said: 'I thought it was pretty funny. I thought that I was going to burp and suddenly I threw up.'

Nausea aside, Murray's admirable courage and new-found stamina in victory went some way to silencing his army of doubters, although Murray conceded that he would have to complete another five-set success for the whispers about his suspect fitness to fade away. It was, according to the shattered Scotsman: 'My best win, or the one that I've enjoyed the most.'

John McEnroe, Murray's cheerleader-in-chief in the media, insisted that the Scot's all-round performance, his instinctive flair for tennis and terrific potential suggested that he was on course for a Top 20 spot in time for the 2006 US Open. McEnroe, who practised with Murray prior to his second round match, delivered the following verdict on Andrew: 'He has a natural feel of how to play the game. He keeps players off balance, he's smart, and that can't be coached. There are a lot of players who are strong and can hit a big ball but he's got a natural feel for movement and when to pick his shots.'

However, talk of Top 20 rankings and trophies

would have to be put on hold if Murray was not able to negotiate his way through a second-round clash with France's Arnaud Clement, an Australian Open finalist in 2001 and former Top 10 player.

The match saw two players of very similar styles come together. The diminutive Frenchman Clement's game is centred on counter-punching from the baseline like Murray, and he covers the court with impressive speed. The Scot, the youngest Briton ever to appear at the US Open, noted before the game: 'He is also intelligent and I'm going to have to play a patient match. I will have to make sure that I don't go for too much, too early, but instead wait for the right opportunity. It should be a fun match to play as we both like to use angles, but I am taller than him so I will probably be hitting the ball harder.'

Murray also believed that he was now benefiting from a more relaxed approach to matches, curbing his inclination to become uptight and flustered when things went wrong, which drained him emotionally. Unfortunately, the one thing Murray had not yet been able to address was his inexperience at playing in five-set matches, and he went down 6-2 7-6 2-6 6-7 6-0 to Clement.

In a manner that mirrored his Wimbledon exit to David Nalbandian, Murray made a whirlwind start, racing into a two-set lead, and then proceeded to wilt as fatigue, Clement's unerring hitting from the baseline and, finally, and most devastatingly, cramp, all took their toll. By the end, Murray was a hobbling, dispirited figure, the complete antithesis of the zestful, inspirational player that had started the match.

As his legs wearied, Murray's temper worsened and he began to question the umpire's calls with increasing vehemence. Although prone to fruity language himself in his pomp, John McEnroe has since claimed that his on-court outbursts, tirades and tantrums often had a counter-productive effect on his game, causing him to lose focus and waste energy. Supermac therefore advised the passionate youth to in future channel his energies into a more aggressive approach in the early stages of a match.

He cautioned: 'Murray has a tendency to feel his way into matches. I think he could do better because he has the ability to get opponents off balance, which, if he came in, would enable him to cut off shots. He gets people in trouble and then he steps back and jerks them around, playing 20-shot rallies that he could bring to a halt inside eight.'

The bitter pain of defeat was exacerbated by the knowledge that the teenager would have realised his season-long goal of entering the Top 100 – and that victory would also have guaranteed him a place at the Australian Open in January 2006.

On the positive side, once the disappointment had faded Murray could take some comfort from the fact that he at least stood on the threshold of a Top 100 spot, at 111. Adopting a more philosophical tone after his courtside histrionics, Murray reflected that: 'I've learned a lot about myself the last three months, and about my tennis and what I need to work on. I'm going to do that when I get the time off at the end of the year.'

Immediately after the US Open Murray was able to take a well-earned break from the pursuit of individual goals and prizes by representing his country against Switzerland in the Davis Cup. Being surrounded by team mates, coaches and fans

Like mentor John McEnroe, Andy Murray has no qualms about remonstrating with the umpire if he feels hard done by.

was just what Murray needed after a tough couple of months on tour.

Yet this was only a short reprieve. Days later Andrew was heading for Bangkok, to take part in the Thailand Open. As ever, vital ranking points were at stake. His first round opponent was George Bastl, who he had already overcome at Wimbledon earlier that summer. Sure enough, Murray triumphed 6-2 6-4. This left Murray just one win away from what he craved the most – a Top 100 ranking.

Nothing was going to stop him now, certainly not world number 41 Robin Soderling, who was edged out 7-6 7-6 by Murray the centurion. 'It's a pretty big deal for me, getting to the Top 100 when I'm 18,' declared the elated youngster. The match itself was a tense affair. Murray, as usual, endured his customary on-court breakdowns and medical pit-stops. This match's complaint was a sore head, which made a pleasant change at least from the cramping legs or liquidating bowels. Encouragingly, Murray found ways to vary his game more than usual, mixing up his shots and deliberately playing to his opponent's weaknesses. At times, Murray may have come across as a schoolboy with a sore tummy trying to get a day off school, but he was definitely maturing tactically. The long slog of the senior tour was having its effect on the young man and teaching him a new trick or two.

'THE SIGNS WERE ALWAYS THERE THAT ANDY WOULD BECOME A TOP-CLASS PLAYER.'

Jeremy Bates on Andrew Murray's elevation into the Top 100

Murray's elevation into the Top 100 led British Davis Cup captain Jeremy Bates to declare: 'It's a big boost to everyone but most of all for Andy himself. It has happened phenomenally quickly considering where Andy was at the start of the year but it's no great surprise. The signs were always there that Andy would become a top-class player.'

But there was no time for Murray to rest on his laurels. There was the small matter of his quarter-final match against the flamboyant American, Robby Ginepri. Murray's pulsating 4-6 6-4 6-3 win over one of the US Open semi-finalists guaranteed him both a further rankings climb and his first ATP tour semi-final.

The prospect of playing Paradorn Srichaphan, Thailand's most revered sportsman, in front of his legions of fanatical fans was daunting to say the least. At least, it should have been. Instead Murray, demonstrating that he was no respecter of reputations, opted to go on the attack and defy the rankings and the odds. His 6-7 7-5 6-2 win over world number 51 Srichaphan was quite simply awe-inspiring. Despite losing the first set on a tie-break,

Fearless Murray was to take on and sensationally beat the Thai Paradon Srichaphan in his homeland in 2005.

Murray fought back tigerishly in the second set, shrugging off the need to call for a trainer to see to a wrist injury and breaking Srichiphan in the 12th game to take the set 7-5.

One set apiece and all to play for. The final set promised to be a cracker. Sadly, for the home crowd at least, it was not to be. Srichaphan became troubled by muscular problems in his left leg and Murray took full advantage, making his ailing opponent pay with ruthless efficiency and precise execution.

The match over, Murray preferred not to bask in the afterglow of success but rather look forward to a dream final against the awesome Roger Federer. 'It's great,' said Murray with characteristic understatement of his impending meeting with the world's most accomplished player. 'Hopefully, I'll get off to a good start. To play against Federer, the best player in the world and possibly one of the greatest ever, at 18 in my first ATP final is a dream come true. I've just got to go out there and try to concentrate at the start and really go for it.'

The odds were heavily stacked against a Murray win. Federer had won his previous 23 final appearances and the evidence suggested that he was unlikely to lose this one. The one thing Murray had in his favour was that he had nothing to lose. As was his natural inclination anyway, he just had to go for it.

There were those who suggested that it was not worth Murray's while to turn up. He had already lost the game weeks ago, when he and Greg Rusedski played against Federer and Yves Allegro in a Davis Cup doubles match. After losing the match, Murray had told Federer that it had been 'an honour' to play him. How could he hope to put up a fight, the critics argued, with such a cowering, deferential attitude to his opponent?

In reality, the Scot was simply paying respect where it was due. At the same time as acknowledging Federer's skill, Murray was also quietly confident of his own abilities.

Once the final got underway Murray found himself uncharacteristically affected by nerves. He dropped his first service game and Federer, with his shark-like ability to sniff out weakness in an opponent and go in for the kill, duly seized the initiative and took the first set 6-3. So far, so easy. But in the next set Murray showed he was made of sterner stuff. He pulled out all the stops and fought toe-to-toe with the Swiss genius. He showcased his sizzling shot-making skills, effortless power and bamboozling spin to break Federer's mighty serve in the sixth game of the second set, having been broken himself in the opening game.

Federer's greater experience of tight situations proved crucial, however, as his aggressive hitting finally wore down the resolve of the doughty Dunblane youth and he was able to grind out the second set 7-5, taking the match in straight sets.

On paper, the Federer express had hurtled on its inexorable path to history: this was his 31st straight win, the longest winning streak since Thomas Muster in 1995; but the Murray motor had also made significant ground in its hunt for perpetual improvement and advancement. At 72 in the men's rankings, he was now remarkably contemplating a passage to the ranks of the Top 50.

As is his wont, Murray was the master of dourness and calm comment after the final. He told reporters: 'I feel good – I played a pretty solid match. I maybe could have returned a little bit better in the first set but it was always going to be tough. It was intimidating playing someone like Roger Federer. I was a little nervous at the start but once I got going it was OK.'

'THAT WAS A VERY TOUGH FINAL TODAY. HE WAS MAKING ME WORK EXTREMELY HARD IN THE END. ANDY WILL BECOME A GOOD PLAYER, I AM SURE OF THAT,'
Roger Federer after the 2005 Thailand Open final

Federer, meanwhile, confessed that he had been severely tested by his game opponent: 'That was a very tough final today. He was making me work extremely hard in the end. It could have suddenly become a really dangerous match for me. Andy will become a good player, I am sure of that. I also lost my first final when I made it onto the tour. This time he had to face the number one in the world, but it is great experience for him.'

Given Murray's age, it is useful to contrast his progress with that of other tennis stars at the same stage of their development. Federer, for example, at 18 had cracked the Top 100 but had only reached one ATP semi-final. The highpoint of Tim Henman's 19th year was reaching the quarter-finals of the Bristol Challenger event. Andre Agassi went one better than Murray, winning his first ATP title aged just 17. He also reached the semi-finals of both the French and US Opens, whereas Murray's best showing was his third-round match at Wimbledon and second-round at the US Open. And Andy Roddick was, like Murray, ranked in the world's Top 200 shortly after his 18th birthday and had also won the junior US Open title. But he went no further than an ATP quarter-final until he was 19.

Mons, Belgium, and the Ethias Trophy, represented Murray's next opportunity for further advancement, and once again the redoubtable Scot's powers of recovery were in evidence when he played his first-round match less than two days after his final in Thailand. He outgunned the Swiss Ivo Heuberger 6-4, 6-4, before claiming a 7-5, 6-3 victory over Gregory Carraz of France in the second round.

Unfortunately, injury intervened for Murray against home favourite Xavier Malisse in the third round, when he suffered a pulled left hamstring while trailing by a set to nil. He was advised to take a 10-day break, giving him a chance to recover and contemplate his next move.

That next move was scheduled to be a momentous one, as it was no less than a first-round match against Tim Henman at the Swiss indoor event at the end of October 2005. It was the game every British tennis fan wanted to see.

CHAPTER 8

THE CHANGING OF THE GUARD

FOR THE casual, non-British tennis observer, a first-round match in the Davidoff Swiss Open in October 2005 would carry little significance.

As a half-empty St. Jakobshalle stadium in Basel bore telling testimony, the Swiss tennis public, intoxicated by the feats of their world number one Roger Federer, were distinctly indifferent to a meeting of Britain's top two men's tennis players, Tim Henman and Andrew Murray. But for the players themselves, the UK public, and the attendant media pack from Britain, this was an era-defining match. It would show if it was time for a change of the guard.

For Murray, it was the chance to play against one of his boyhood heroes. Henman had been the standard bearer of British tennis for a decade, lionised and criticised in equal measure for his

annual courageous failures at Wimbledon, as well
as the other oh-so-close attempts to win at major
and Grand Slam tournaments.

For tennis aficionados in Britain the tie offered a
study in contrasts. It was Scotland v England for a
start; and the punishing base-line specialist against
the wily serve-volleyer; finally, of course, it was the
rising star taking on the fading force.

Before the match, Murray talked down his chances,

**Murray would announce his youthful presence in
October 2005 when he beat Tim Henman in three
sets at the Swiss Masters.**

preferring instead to lavish praise on his opponent: 'It is a match I'm looking forward to. I have great respect for Tim as a man and as a tennis player. He has a great career and he will be quite a challenge to play him.' Ever the gentleman, Henman returned the compliment, saying: 'It's the first time I've played Andy but I'm not going to approach it any differently. I'll go out there knowing the way I want to play. One of us is going to win and one of us is going to lose but it won't be the be-all and end-all. When we step on court we'll do everything we can to

The match against Henman was a chance for Murray to play against one of his idols.

win but, in the context of the whole year for both of us, I don't think it will have that big an impact.'

Nice try Tim, but no one was ever going to buy that! Such was the importance of this tantalising tussle that the BBC overhauled its whole afternoon schedule to cover the match live. Fans of daytime cookery and makeover shows were forced to forego their daily diet of dishes and DIY for one day as tennis fever gripped the nation.

'IT'S BEEN ONE-WAY TRAFFIC SO FAR. WE'VE SEEN MORE MONEY ON MURRAY THIS WEEK THAN WE SAW IN THE WHOLE OF WIMBLEDON FORTNIGHT. MURRAY-MANIA HAS HIT OUR SHOPS,'

A Ladbrokes spokesman on the eve of the first-ever Murray-Henman match

The bookmakers had a field day, too, as the confrontation loomed. A Murray win was the popular bet for many punters – one of whom splashed out £15,000 on a Henman defeat. A Ladbrokes spokesman said at the time: 'It's been one-way traffic so far. We've seen more money on Murray this week than we saw in the whole of Wimbledon fortnight. Murray-mania has hit our shops.'

Perhaps inevitably with a match so incessantly hyped beforehand, the tie billed as the Battle of

Britain turned into something of a phony war. In the event, it was a scrappy, tentative affair that failed to live up to its lofty expectations. Of the two protagonists, Murray seemed less affected by the enormous significance of the encounter than his more experienced opponent and former practice partner. He stormed to the first set in commanding style, taking it 6-2 in just 34 minutes after breaking his compatriot in the first game.

Displaying a rich repertoire of shots, Murray was also the more consistent of the pair in the first set, making just 11 unforced errors to his struggling opponent's 25. Living up to his 'Tiger Tim' nickname, Henman fought back to take the second set 7-5, but Murray regained his composure and displayed his innate competitiveness to battle through the third to take it 7-6, sealing his brilliant victory with a deft forehand.

'TO WIN AGAINST SOMEONE LIKE THAT, WHO I HAVE SO MUCH RESPECT FOR, WHO INSPIRED ME – IF IT WEREN'T FOR HIM I MIGHT NOT EVEN BE PLAYING – IS A PRETTY BIG DEAL,'

Andrew Murray on Tim Henman

For once, the normally phlegmatic Scot was visibly emotional after the match as he sat at the courtside and fought back the tears. Facing the reporters, he declared: 'It's definitely the biggest win of my career. This is a pretty special day for me and I'll remember it for the rest of my life. I have so much respect for him and it's always tough when you feel like that going into a match. He is one of the best players in the last 10 years and to win against him is just amazing. I can't really describe how I feel. I tried not to show so much emotion during the match out of respect for Tim but at the end I couldn't hold it in any more. To win against someone like that, who I have so much respect for, who inspired me – if it weren't for him I might not even be playing – is a pretty big deal.'

The gritty, tenacious Scot had, by virtue of a thrilling three-set triumph, supplanted his passive English counterpart as the new beacon of hope for UK tennis. It was, simply, a seismic shift in power in British men's tennis. While Murray was still 42 ranking places below Henman – the Scot had leapt to 70 in the world rankings while the Englishman had slumped from six to 28 – it was self-evident that sooner rather than later the teenager would overtake his older rival. This was especially true as, on top of advancing age, a degenerative back condition began to affect Henman more and more.

Commentators hoped that Murray's win would signal a revival in interest in tennis in the UK.

Murray's momentous win over Henman would spark a renewed interest in British tennis just as Swedes embraced the game with stars such as Stefan Edberg.

Henman, for all his achievements, had essentially failed to spark mass public interest beyond British tennis's traditional middle-class support. Murray seemed much more a man of the people, or, more accurately, a normal kid, the kind you see hanging around shopping malls on any Saturday of the year. In the same way that Björn Borg's exploits in the late 1970s had inspired a generation of young Swedes to take up tennis – such as Mats Wilander and Stefan Edberg – it was hoped that Murray's rise would inspire his contemporaries to do the same.

> **'Dunblane's finest doesn't give a stuff for reputations. He isn't about to be cowed by an opponent just because he's got 10 years on him,'**
>
> *The People* newspaper on Andrew Murray

The People newspaper claimed the Scot as one of their own, a real tennis player for real people: 'Dunblane's finest doesn't give a stuff for reputations. He isn't about to be cowed by an opponent just because he's got 10 years on him. If the ball's there, hit it. If it comes back, hit it harder. If it doesn't come back, celebrate with all the emotion you can muster and live for the moment.' It is difficult to imagine any newspaper ever saying that about Tim Henman.

Naturally, Murray's vanquishing of a Sassenach was warmly welcomed by his fellow Scots, with the tabloid newspaper *The Daily Record* going as far as hailing his victory as the sixth most memorable milestone in Scottish sporting history.

Perhaps the only people who didn't celebrate Murray's win were the bookmakers. William Hill paid out to Murray's supporters in what had been the first-ever £1 million-backed tennis game outside of the Wimbledon final. One punter placed a bet of £13,500 on Murray to win, while other sums included £11,000 and £4,000. Unsurprisingly, William Hill immediately shortened Murray's odds for future tournaments, including making him 11/8 to be British number one at the end of 2006; Henman was rated at 7/4 and Greg Rusedski 2/1.

The Scot was also installed at 25/1 to win Wimbledon in 2006, with Henman at 33/1 and a meeting of the pair in the final at SW19 rated at 400/1. Greg Rusedski's odds were fixed at 80/1. Furthermore, William Hill drew up odds of 12/1 that the emerging youngster would win a Grand Slam tournament in 2006 and 3/1 on him to do so before the end of 2010.

Following his energy-sapping, mentally-draining performance against Henman, Murray progressed to a meeting with Tomas Berdych, the Czech world number 52. Grit and determination saw him grind out a hard-earned 6-4 2-6 6-4 victory,

Having beaten Tomas Berdych, Murray was free to go to the semi-finals.

which confirmed that, unlike many British players of the past, Murray was capable of commendable consistency.

Barring Murray's passage into the semi-finals of the tournament was the formidable figure of Chilean fourth seed and world number 17 Fernando Gonzalez. Murray opined that he would have to play his best-ever match if he were to cause another upset. The mercurial South American possesses one of the most venomous weapons on the men's tour, a savage forehand — which he unleashed with an awesome regularity that initially bewildered the Scot. A dazzling array of drop shots also confounded the teenage tyro, as the Chilean blitzed his opponent to take the first set 6-4.

Murray's steely resolve was not to buckle, however, and he battled his way back into contention, aided by a rash of mistakes from a wayward González. The Scot set up a deciding set by prevailing 6-3 in the second, before the Chilean reasserted control and fired winner after winner from his smouldering racket to take the final set 6-1.

'I SUPPOSE IT'S A GOOD SIGN WHEN YOU'RE BEATING TOP 50 PLAYERS WITHOUT PLAYING YOUR BEST TENNIS.'

Andrew Murray gets cocky

It was Fernando Gonzalez who put an end to Andy's Swiss Masters hopes.

Murray expressed his disappointment at not being able to cope with the powerful South American, although he added: 'But I suppose it's a good sign when you're beating Top 50 players without playing your best tennis.'

When he reflected on his Swiss sojourn in more depth, Murray could be extremely gratified that he had not only edged his world ranking closer to the magical 50 mark – he was now placed 67 – but that he had also crept ever-closer to the summit of British tennis. Although the world rankings said otherwise, Murray was now Britain's top tennis player

The king (aka Tim Henman) was dead, long live the king...

CHAPTER 9

FLOWER OF SCOTLAND

WHEN AN American interviewer incorrectly referred to Andrew Murray as English during Wimbledon 2005 he was rebuked immediately: 'No, I'm Scottish!' barked Dunblane's favourite son. It is a truth universally acknowledged in these Isles that, while he is winning, Andrew Murray is British; once he begins to lose he will henceforth be referred to as: 'Scotland's Andy Murray'!

But no matter what people think of him, Andrew Murray sees himself as a Scot – and a proud one at that. And the Scots are proud of him, too.

One reason for this was surely the dreadful dearth of Scottish sporting talent in 2005. Andrew Murray could not fail to stand out in what was a pretty empty field. The Scots, therefore, cherish every morsel of Scottish sporting success with considerable ardour, knowing that they may not see its like again for an interminable age.

Both the country's football and rugby teams have toiled relentlessly but fruitlessly for meagre success, while, save for the odd Olympic curling success (in 2002) and a Stephen Hendry or John Higgins' win in the World Snooker Championships, Scottish sports fans have not had a great deal to cheer about in recent years. In this situation, the stage was set for a new Scottish sporting icon to emerge, and in 2005 Andrew Murray did just that.

A Scottish fan celebrates a rarity – a successful Scottish sportsman: Andrew Barron Murray.

What made Murray's emergence all the sweeter for Scots was that here was one of their own proving a success in tennis, a game traditionally considered the preserve of the English middle classes. Scotland could never truly embrace Britain's blue-eyed boy, Tim Henman, the very personification of Englishness with his neatly coiffured, jet-black hair and reserved on-court demeanour – a man who Murray would supplant as British number one in February 2006, the first Scot to achieve such a distinction.

> **'So near, so far.'**
>
> *The Scotsman* newspaper neatly sums up the history of Scottish sport

What a contrast Murray offered to Henman. Animated, aggressive and passionate, he could not have been more different from his English counterpart. His appearance was something to behold, too, his straggly hair and usually grimacing face making him look like nothing less than a modern-day Braveheart. No wonder the Scots could not resist him.

Little do most people know it, but Scotland has a long history in tennis going way back to its very beginnings. Although the game is thought to have emerged in 12th century France, Scotland can in fact lay claim to the world's oldest playing arena, the Royal Tennis Court at Falkland. James V built the court in 1539 in the grounds of Falkland Palace, Fife, the royal hunting lodge of the Stewarts. It is believed that as well as James V, Mary Queen of Scots and James VI (James I of England) also played on the Royal Tennis Court. The court was completed in 1541, and to this day it has changed little. In 1989, royalty returned to the Royal Court at Falkland Palace when, to celebrate its 450th anniversary, an international tournament was held there in which Prince Edward took part, watched by the Queen.

Fast forward to 2005 and, not only did Murray impress Scots everywhere by displaying traditional Caledonian virtues of grit and determination, there was a touch of the Scottish tragic hero in his mesmeric rise and injury-induced falls.

Scotland has become inured to heroic failure in the sporting domain – the excruciating agony of Gary McAllister and Gavin Hastings' penalty misses for Scotland against England at football and rugby respectively spring readily to mind – and Andy Murray served up more of the same during an unforgettable summer.

It was almost inevitable that a surfeit of optimism in the Scot's memorable Wimbledon campaign, in which he became the first Scot to successfully negotiate the first round since Winnie Shaw in 1976, would be superseded by pain and anguish in the aftermath of glorious defeat.

Writing in the *Scotsman*, Alan Pattullo painted

Murray strived to show he was not just prone to the archetypal bad luck of Scottish sportsmen which sometimes afflicted the likes of Gary McAllister, who missed a penalty for Scotland against England in the 1996 European Championships.

Murray as a kind of Scottish everyman during his match with David Nalbandian:

Murray certainly benefited from the energy spilling down from the box, and almost every seat in the house. Poor Nalbandian. Tossed on a partisan wave into an environment featuring See You Jimmy hats and saltire-painted faces, his every fault was cheered with a tennis equivalent of the Hampden Roar. But if Scotland's national football stadium had been evoked, then so had the ghosts of too many Scottish let downs of the past. Murray slipped into the shoes of Billy Bremner, who missed with the goal at his mercy against Brazil in the 1974 World Cup. He followed that same anguished tread which has haunted Scottish football, from Don Masson's 1978 penalty miss in Argentina to a repeat by Gary McAllister at Wembley in 1996. So near, so far.

Yet Murray is different, he is no perennially under-achieving Scot and does not come out in a cold sweat when words such as 'triumph', 'victory' and 'success' are used in close proximity to the word 'Scottish'.

Andrew Murray readily talks about his ambition to do well, about his desire to move up the rankings and win tournaments. When in interviews he says things like, 'When I make the Top 10 in the next two or three years...', it is not arrogance, merely what the Scots call 'gallus', the cocky confidence of someone who knows that they are good and is not afraid to show it.

In November 2005, Murray was given the opportunity of putting one over on the Auld Enemy when a Scotland v England tennis challenge was staged in Aberdeen, at the city's AECC Press and

Journal Arena. This keenly-awaited tussle also featured an intriguing sub-plot as it pitted Murray, Britain's number three, against a man one place higher in his country's rankings: Greg Rusedski.

As the much-anticipated conflict with the auld enemy loomed, staunchly Scottish website The Jaggy Thistle: Scotland the Barbed comically captured the mood of a nation – beat England at all costs:

'Apart from his ubiquitous mum, on hand to take dirt off his face with a spit and wipe while Andy says "Mum, stop it! People are watching!", Andy confirmed that Hamish, the family labrador, will also support our brave boys in their quest to stuff the Devil Spawn Of Satan. In an unusual move, Hamish will patrol Andy's side of the court, ready to neutralise kid-on Canuck Rusedski's ferocious serve, by jumping up, grabbing the ball in mid-air and then charging round the court like a daftie before dropping the ball at Andy's feet while wagging his tail furiously.

'ONE OF THE THINGS I WANT TO DO AS A TENNIS PLAYER FROM SCOTLAND IS RAISE THE SPORT'S PROFILE.'

Andrew Murray, patriot

The Scottish wonder was well aware that he was carrying the weight of a nation's expectations on his

Murray demonstrates his commitment to his country's cause during the Aberdeen Cup in which Scotland and England clash in November 2005.

shoulders. He said: 'One of the things I want to do as a tennis player from Scotland is raise the sport's profile. We haven't had many high-profile players before, and we have a chance to make tennis into a pretty big game. As a sportsman, you never want to lose anything, and I certainly don't want to lose against England. I am sure the rest of the guys in the team are thinking the same.'

As the tournament played out, Murray got his wish. With the match finely poised, Murray defeated his Canadian-born English opponent 4-6 6-4 7-6, aided in no small part by a calf injury to Rusedski. The result helped Scotland to a 4.5-2.5 win over England. It would be unfair to suggest that

Murray's win was solely down to Rusedski's injury – it had as much to do with his in-built fighting nature and in his desire to avenge his defeat against Rusedski the previous day.

In securing the inaugural Aberdeen Cup for Scotland, Murray praised Rusedski and the rest of the England team. Rusedski responded by congratulating Murray on capitalising on his calf injury – it displayed a necessary ruthless streak that young Scot needed in order to get on. He commented: 'That's a good sign. We want to see players showing no mercy.'

Murray's inspiring alliance with brother Jamie was also instrumental in Scotland's success, as the Murray boys teamed up to prevail over Rusedski and David Sherwood in the doubles, while Scottish female number one, Elena Baltacha, Joanna Henderson and Scott Lister also contributed to what was truly a collective team effort.

Scotland's victory in the Aberdeen Cup had an electrifying effect on the nation. With Andrew Murray cast as the Pied Piper, suddenly young children were rushing out to tennis courts to emulate their hero. Mike Kolacz of Glasgow City Council, the body that administers the Scotstoun and Govan tennis Centres, is one person who certainly noticed the change. He commented at the time: 'This summer there has been a definite upturn in numbers since Andy Murray burst on the scene. There is a buzz about tennis definitely, and a number of the coaches working with us have remarked on this. The impact of Murray has been very positive. The interest in tennis here is unprecedented.' Scotland is a nation with some of the highest levels of obesity in the world, and any event which had the country's young rushing out to take part in sport can only be applauded.

And it wasn't just in Glasgow that the people of Scotland were following Murray's example. Ian Woodcraft, rackets manager of the Next Generation in Monifieth – where Murray's mother Judy once worked before moving on to become national coach – noticed how Murray's successes supercharged every generation of tennis player, and not just the kids at the club. He says: 'Andrew Murray's successes have certainly had an effect. We have children as young as 3 and one adult in his 80s, who play, and they are all, throughout the age spectrum, talking about Andy; they are positively raving about him. You hear the

> **'You hear the children here talking about him all the time. I think it helps that he is of their generation and has a more rebellious image than someone like Tim Henman.'**
>
> Scottish tennis club manager Ian Woodcraft on Andrew Murray

children here talking about him all the time. I think it helps that he is of their generation and has a more rebellious image than someone like Tim Henman.'

Throughout the country, tennis clubs reported soaring membership applications, while private coaches were busier than they had ever been before.

Another knock-on benefit of the Murray Effect is that, after years of neglect, suddenly public money was made available to Scottish sport. It also helped that Judy Murray actively lobbied influential figures in government to encourage them to overcome their traditional parsimoniousness and loosen their purse strings.

Murray indulges in a spot of head tennis during the Aberdeen Cup.

In October 2005, Scotland's sports minister Patricia Ferguson announced that £293,000, funded by Sportscotland, the country's national sport agency, would be invested in the country's tennis players. The cash injection would finance both the coaching and development of young players, but would also support existing players such as Murray himself. Distributed through a series of grants and aid, the money would go some way towards helping Scotland's tennis clubs in rearing the next generation of Andrew Murrays.

Jim Campbell, chief executive of Tennis Scotland, anounced: 'We are very excited about the future of the sport in this country and we are absolutely delighted with the investment being made by Sportscotland. The success of Andrew Murray, as well as other top Scottish players, is incredible and undoubtedly will inspire youngsters to take up the sport.'

In February 2006, there was further evidence of a renaissance in Scottish sport. Oil tycoon Sir Bill Gammell, chief executive of Cairn Energy, announced plans to establish the Scottish Institute of Sport Foundation, whose mission would be to help the best athletes to reach the pinnacle of their sport. The Perthshire-born multi-millionaire personally pledged £275,000 to the project. Its aim, he said, was to instil a winning mindset into Scots sportsmen and women. Would any of these developments have occurred without the exploits of Andrew Murray? Probably not.

So look out world. By the time the London Olympics rolls around in 2012, not to mention the possibility of a Commonwealth Games held in Glasgow in 2014, expect a disproportionate number of medals to be heading north of the border.

As Murray Mania swept across Scotland, tennis entered the previously uncharted territory of the playgrounds of the country's primary schools. A new initiative called Ariel was launched in September 2005, a game of mini-tennis designed to capture the imagination of the younger generation. With the emphasis as much on fun as competition, Ariel allows players to progress through red, orange and green stages before advancing on to full tennis when their strength and ability permits.

'WHEN I ASK THEM WHO THEIR FAVOURITE PLAYER IS THEY DON'T SAY ANDY RODDICK OR ROGER FEDERER ANYMORE: THEY SAY ANDY MURRAY BECAUSE HE'S SCOTTISH.'

Ryan Hargreaves, an Edinburgh tennis coach on his experience of young Scottish tennis fans

Greg Rusedski (left) Andy Murray pose with their trophies in the November 2005 Aberdeen Cup.

Ryan Hargreaves, a tennis coach who works with primary school children in Edinburgh, admits: 'There has been huge interest from kids since Wimbledon. When I ask them who their favourite player is they don't say Andy Roddick or Roger Federer anymore: they say Andy Murray because he's Scottish and they've seen him playing on TV. But at the moment we go into some schools and they still have poor plastic rackets that have been lying around for years so we provide all the kit and carry it from school to school. If there was mini-tennis equipment in primaries they could play more and not have to rely on coaches.'

Inevitably, the politicians tried to get in on the act and bask in some of the reflected glory of Murray's achievements. Scottish minister Bruce Crawford even asked that the Scottish Parliament 'Recognises the superb effort made by Scots tennis player Andrew Murray from Dunblane in reaching the third round of this year's Wimbledon tennis tournament; applauds him for the skill, tenacity and maturity that he displayed throughout the tournament which will stand him good stead as he goes on to represent Scotland and win major grand slam tennis tournaments in the future.' Crawford then went on to castigate the Scottish Executive for its chronic under funding of Scottish sport and urged it to dig deep in order to raise a new generation of Scottish sporting heroes. Vote for me – I like Andrew Murray!

The last word on the matter, though, should be left with Murray: 'Our national football and rugby teams have been struggling in recent years so it's nice everyone is suddenly talking about a tennis player because Scotland has never been a hot-bed of tennis before. If I can inspire other kids to take up the game then that's brilliant.'

CHAPTER 10

BRITISH BULLDOG

THE DAVIS Cup has always been a vitally important event for British tennis players, a tournament where they can put aside their personal ambitions and rivalries, and play together as a team, drawing on each other for inspiration and support. Self-obsessive individual goals and challenges are set aside for a weekend rich in drama, tension and sumptuous, high-octane sporting entertainment.

Inspired by the formidable Fred Perry, Great Britain last won the competition in 1936, completing a memorable run of four successive victories.

Andrew Murray's first taste of Davis Cup action came in 2005. Aged just 17, he made history by becoming the youngest Briton ever to take part in the tournament. It was a winning debut, too. Matched up against Israel, he was teamed with

Murray has a long way to go before he can match the peerless Davis Cup record of Fred Perry (left), here with Gottfried von Cramm at Wimbledon in 1931.

David Sherwood in the doubles and together the youthful pair secured an unforgettable victory.

Just one year previously, Murray had joined the British squad in Luxembourg for their country's Euro-African zone tie. Murray was delighted at being given such a valuable opportunity by British Davis Cup captain Jeremy Bates to enhance his development. The recognition was particularly pleasing for Murray given that, at the time, he was sidelined with a serious knee injury and naturally depressed and frustrated. 'It's been great for me,' he confessed. 'Being around Tim and Greg has been excellent, both at practice and at dinner. Both of them are really nice people, so easy to get on with. I'd seen them a couple of times and said "hi," but never for more than two or three minutes. I couldn't believe how nice they were when I first met them.'

Only a matter of months later, in September 2004, Murray's continued progress, including his success

British Davis Cup captain Jeremy Bates talks to Andy (left) and Greg Rusedski during their Davis Cup play-off doubles match against Switzerland in September 2005.

in securing the US Open junior crown, saw him rewarded with a call-up to Britain's squad for the match against Austria. His brilliant form, allied to the fact that the World Group qualifier was to be played on clay – a surface on which Murray flourishes – meant he stood an excellent chance of being blooded against Austria.

'TECHNICALLY, HE HAD FANSTASTIC HAND SKILL, GOOD TIMING AND RACKET-HEAD SPEED... ONE OF HIS BIGGEST ATTRIBUTES IS THAT HE UNDERSTANDS VERY CLEARLY HOW TO HURT SOMEBODY AND WHERE THE GAPS ARE,'

Jeremy Bates on Andrew Murray

Team captain Jeremy Bates certainly indicated that he had no qualms about using the Scot if necessary. He told one newspaper:

He hates losing and takes great enjoyment out of beating people. He wants to become a good professional and is not remotely carried away by winning the US Open title. He sees it for what it is – a stepping stone. It's terrific to be working with somebody who has the whole thing in perspective. Technically, he has fantastic hand skill, good timing and racket-head speed. His technique is solid from the ground, and one of his biggest attributes is that he understands very clearly how to hurt somebody and where the gaps are. He has the ability to open up the court and put the ball where the other guy doesn't like it. He reads the game well and can use all his skills on clay because it's like a game of chess out there.

Although Murray was eventually overlooked for selection against the Austrians, Britain's 3-2 defeat and subsequent relegation to the Euro-Africa zone looked set to guarantee his inclusion in his country's next Davis Cup team. Both the Dunblane youngster and Alex Bogdanovic had been groomed to replace ageing stalwarts Tim Henman and Greg Rusedski, who were badly in need of some youthful assistance in their Davis Cup heroics.

However, most tennis pundits advised against tossing Murray and Bogdanovic into the fray too soon against more experienced opponents given their lack of experience in the professional arena. Yet, when Tim Henman announced his unexpected retirement from Davis Cup action in January 2005, Murray's debut in the cut-and-thrust of prestigious international competition moved ever closer.

There was little surprise, therefore, that three months later Murray, Bogdanovic, Greg Rusedski

Andy Murray and David Sherwood after their Davis Cup tennis match in Ramat Hasharon against Israel's Andy Ram and Jonathan Erlich.

and David Sherwood were announced as Britain's team for the Davis Cup trip to Israel.

Murray was handed a baptism of fire in the doubles with David Sherwood. He duly became his country's youngest-ever Davis Cup player, aged 17 and 294 days, eclipsing the record set by 18-year-old Roger Becker in 1952.

The dynamic young duo's opponents in Tel Aviv were Andy Ram and Jonathan Erlich who, although not exactly household names, were are the time ranked the eighth best doubles partnership in the world. Going into the game the tie was delicately poised at one match each. Murray and Sherwood knew that a vital win in the doubles would decisively tip the balance Britain's way.

Greg Rusedski was a heavy favourite to prevail against Noam Okun, the Israeli number one, in the reverse singles. This meant that all the pressure was placed on Murray and Sherwood, the perceived weak link in the British chain.

Jeremy Bates had taken the brave decision to omit Rusedski from the doubles in order to conserve his energy for the two singles matches he would have to play. Bates's tactical foresight was rewarded by the British pair in a remarkable performance by a

Murray joins up with the Great Britain squad (from left to right captain Jeremy Bates, Greg Rusedski and Tim Henman) for the Davis Cup clash with Austria in September 2004.

guileful Murray and a razor-sharp Sherwood. Playing like a couple of Davis Cup veterans, Murray and Sherwood bulldozed their way to a two-set lead, 6-4 7-6.

Inevitably, the Israelis fought back, sealing the third set 2-6 as Murray and Sherwood struggled to maintain their momentum. The Israelis attempted to dominate the early stages of the fourth set, too, breaking Sherwood's serve to the deafening delight of the partisan 5,000-strong crowd.

But cometh the hour, cometh the wonderboy. Refusing to back down, Andrew Murray unleashed his arsenal of spectacular returns, inspirational leadership and cut-throat competitiveness. Throughout the peaks and troughs of this scintillating, seesawing encounter, Murray's vociferous encouragement to both himself and his partner kept his country in the tie. A little McEnroe-style belligerence did not go amiss either, as Murray questioned every adverse call. At one point he even mounted the referee's platform to have it out with the official. It was priceless stuff.

When Sherwood and Murray faced three set points at 0-40 and 5-6 down, the Scot demanded they both reach inside their souls to wrench out every last ounce of guts and grit to force a tie-break.

The superlative Scot's encouragement paid off magnificently. Through sheer force of will, Murray and Sherwood won the game and forced the match into a tie break – which they won 7-5.

This was a stunning victory, one of the best in Britain's recent Davis Cup history, and it was in no small part due to Murray and his never-say-die attitude.

> **'I've never been involved in a match like that, either on or off the court. In terms of my Davis Cup experiences, it beats them all. For two guys making their Davis Cup debuts they were inspirational doubles players out there.'**
>
> Jeremy Bates
> after Murray and
> Sherwood's memorable
> Davis Cup doubles
> win against Israel

The ecstatic response by the pair of British lions and their team was almost as memorable as the match that had preceded it. Murray, Sherwood, Bates and other British team members celebrated together in scenes of unbridled jubilation, with Murray's toothy grin providing a memorable highlight.

Britain now had an unassailable lead in the tie, prompting a delighted Murray to remark: 'It was a dream for me to play Davis Cup. I gave 100 per cent and was geed up to help my partner right till the very end.'

A breathless Jeremy Bates gasped afterwards: 'I've never been involved in a match like that, either on or off the court. In terms of my Davis Cup experiences, it beats them all. For two guys making their Davis Cup debuts they were inspirational doubles players out there.'

David Felgate, the LTA's performance director, said waves of optimism had suffused the British side, as he looked forward eagerly to the next enthralling chapter in the thrill-a-minute Davis Cup story. He remarked: 'There will be some very tough teams in the draw, but we've got the right spirit, and if we get the right draw, who knows? There is great team spirit and it's been building over the last year and a half. The difference is now, this isn't just a team that comes together for the Davis Cup, a lot of them practise together.'

Murray was sadly deprived of further Davis Cup delight against Israel when a foot injury ruled him out of the reverse singles, which Greg Rusedski won and David Sherwood lost. However, for sheer excitement, guts, determination and passion this was truly one of the most enjoyable occasions for anyone involved in British tennis. A new and vibrant era had seemingly been heralded for the country's Davis Cup side, which boasted a tightly-knit team combining youth and experience in a powerful, cohesive unit.

At the vanguard of the British renaissance was Andy Murray, whose boundless energy, impressive valour and considerable talent – allied to the experience and wiliness of the big-serving Rusedski

– could in theory drag those around them to a higher level of competitiveness and Davis Cup success.

However, when all the brouhaha had subsided and the hyperbole had ceased, the realisation dawned that Britain still had to prove they could mix it with the world's best. Britain's next encounter, with Switzerland later in 2005, would prove more of a barometer of their standing in the world's elite. For one thing, it meant that they would be up against Roger Federer.

Federer was in a class of his own, and even if he did not see the Davis Cup as his main priority, he was still more than willing to repay the fanatical support of his countrymen by turning out for Switzerland's Davis Cup team.

In September 2005, Britain lined up against Switzerland for their next Davis Cup tie. Naturally, Murray retained his place in the British team, alongside Greg Rusedski and David Sherwood, and another Scot, Alan Mackin.

Mackin had the unenviable mission of attempting to derail the Federer juggernaut in the opening match in Geneva, a nigh-on impossible task. Federer duly dispatched his unfortunate opponent 6-0 6-0 6-2.

It was now up to another Scot, Murray, to rise to the occasion once again and keep the tie alive. He was matched up against Stanislas Wawrinka, the

Swiss number two, who the British saw as Switzerland's weak link considering that he had lost his three previous Davis Cup matches. He was also thought to be prone to nerves and tension during big matches.

Murray and Greg Rusedski put their heads together in Great Britain's Davis Cup tie against Switzerland.

Sadly, Murray was a pale shadow of the pumped-up player that had emerged victorious in Israel. He appeared subdued and impotent as Wawrinka displayed the greater accuracy of shot and more control to claim the first set 6-4.

The Scot upped the tempo in the second set and managed to take it to a tie break, which he eventually lost 7-5. The third set proved pretty routine for the Swiss. Despite being broken once, Wawrinka was able to take Murray's serve twice, to win the set 6-4 and thus sealing the match.

Murray conceded that 20-year-old Wawrinka's 60th place in the world rankings had been the decisive factor. He said: 'I played OK, but I didn't serve as well as I would have wanted and I didn't return as well as I would have wanted. I didn't play well enough to beat him. But I wasn't the favourite to win this match. He is ranked 50 places higher than me and he was playing on his favourite surface.'

It would need a performance of heroic proportions for the British team to now overhaul the Swiss and win the tie. The task of getting Britain back on track fell once again to Murray, this time teamed with Rusedski in a doubles match against Federer and Yves Allegro. The Swiss won the first set 7-5, but Murray and Rusedski rallied to take the second 6-2. After falling behind 5-3 in the third set, the British duo recovered to force a tie-break, which they then meekly surrendered 7-1.

The next set was crucial and, of all people, it was Murray who cracked. His serve was broken twice as Federer and Allegro cruised to a 6-2 win. The match, and the tie, was over. With a 3-0 lead in the tie there was no way that the Swiss could now lose.

Perhaps, in the final analysis, Murray had felt too weighed down by the expectations of his home country. As in the past, his spirit was more than willing but the flesh was weak. He was well below par against Wawrinka, showed flashes of brilliance in the doubles, but despite under-performing had once again displayed that even when his skill levels were inadequate, his commitment and patriotism were unquestionable.

CHAPTER II

GROWING PAINS

IF THERE is one thing worth remembering about Andrew Murray above all else it is that he is still a very young man. Mentally, emotionally and physically, he is still growing. And it is this last aspect of the Scot's development that has attracted the most attention. His frequent physical breakdowns, his extraordinary bout of on-court vomiting at the 2005 US Open and his tendency to cramp have all led some observers to question Andrew Murray's physical suitability to be a top-class tennis player.

So, were the Scot's repeated injury woes a case of teenage growing pains, a fleeting annoyance, or were they evidence of a more long-term worry for this burgeoning young star?

Such were the concerns for Murray's fitness that

he was forced to pay a visit to the famed Institute of Sports Medicine in France at the end of 2005 to investigate his tendency to cramp during matches. Diagnosis revealed that the problem was related to a weak back. Andrew was advised to undertake regular strengthening exercises, much to his relief. As physical problems went, this one wasn't career threatening. The cramping was surely a symptom of Murray's rapid growth over the past couple of years. Once he finished growing, in theory the cramps would stop.

However, as well as his age-related growing pains, what many of Murray's critics did not know was that his genes also predisposed him to certain ailments, regardless of his fitness levels.

For example, Murray was born with a bifurcated – or separated – right knee cap. Rapid growth spurts at the beginning of both 2004 and 2005 put extra pressure on his right knee, which served to exacerbate this already existing condition. In the 2004 instance the result was painful tendinitis, which forced Murray to stop playing for five frustrating months while he slowly recovered. His early 2005 growth spurt – at one point he grew by a centimetre in just seven days – led to severe lower-back pain.

While there is no good time to be injured, it is surely the case that Murray's 2004 and 2005 lay offs could not have come at a worse time. Each occurred precisely at the moment when he was reaching the peak of his form.

This was certainly true when Andrew Murray leapt into the national consciousness with his coruscating appearance at the Stella Artois Championship in June 2005.

Everything appeared to be going well for Murray. He had won his first- and second-round matches and domestic audiences were beginning to sit up and take notice. He entered into his third-round match against former Australian Open champion Thomas Johansson full of confidence.

The match was closely fought, and at one set all and 3-3 in the third it was poised to go either way. Then disaster struck. Just when Murray appeared capable of pulling off another sensational victory in front of his home fans, his body let him down. Assailed from nowhere by paralysing tension he collapsed with cramp in an agonising spasm. As he attempted to play on a beleaguered Murray, attempting a difficult return from the baseline, fell awkwardly on his ankle. Although he later claimed that he had heard something 'crack', Murray submitted himself to lengthy treatment in an effort to patch himself up and carry on. Barely able to walk, let along run, Murray nevertheless refused to retire and he and Johansson played out the rest of

During the third round of the Stella Artois tournament in 2005, Murray collapses in a crumpled heap, twisting his ankle.

the set in perfunctory style, with the Swede eventually winning 7-5.

A post-match scan showed that Murray had only suffered a sprain that would heal in time. However, just a few weeks later at Wimbledon, doubts over his health resurfaced to cast a more lasting cloud of doubt over his ability to withstand the exertions of high-level tennis.

After roaring into a two-set lead over former Wimbledon finalist David Nalbandian in the third round, Murray's failure to seal a three-set win meant that he would have to subject his body to a severe physical examination over four or, as it turned out, five punishing sets. As the game wore on, and Murray's energy levels flagged, he was laid low by cramp once more and Nalbandian drew on his greater reserves of physical strength to take the match. Such was Murray's collapse that he meekly surrendered the third set 6-0. He fought back in the fourth, which he lost 6-4, but offered little resistance in the final set, going down 6-1.

Suddenly, the talk at Wimbledon was not so much about Murray the Wonder Boy as Murray the Weakling. His perceived physical frailty was endlessly discussed in the crowds, the courts, the TV studios and press boxes. Comparisons were drawn between the Scot and Spanish rising star, Rafael Nadal. Where Murray was tall and slender, Nadal

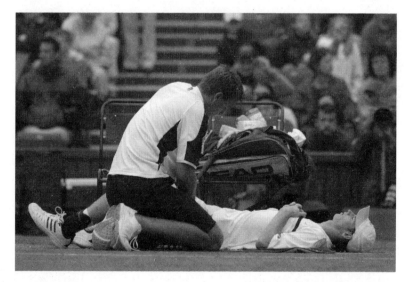

The return of the killer cramp – Murray becomes a victim on the verge of beating the Argentinian David Nalbandian in the third round of Wimbledon 2005.

Rafael Nadal and Andy Murray have been compared as talents.

was squat and muscular; where Murray was gangly and prone to on-court thrills and spills, Nadal was low-slung and well-balanced. It was Nadal, they said, who was built to play tennis; Murray, they argued, was quite simply the wrong shape.

Yet, as Murray's coach Mark Petchey pointed out, despite being a similar age to Nadal – Murray was 18 while Nadal was 19 at the time – the pair were at completely different stages in their physical development. 'Andy is still growing and you have to manage your body differently,' Petchey explained. 'I think it will take another couple of years for him to be fully fit. The signs are he's still got some growing left to do.'

Rafael Nadal stopped growing at 17 and from that point on was able to concentrate on building up his physical strength. Murray, getting taller every day, had to put this sort of training on hold until it was decided that he had stopped growing. His five-month lay-off with tendinitis also inhibited his physical development. In effect, by not playing or training for such a long time, Murray was effectively five months behind his contemporaries.

Dan Thorpe, a Lawn Tennis Association coach, also explained after the Nalbandian match that Murray's sense of excitement may also have contributed to his collapse. As the home favourite, he would have been extremely pumped up, the adrenaline surging through his body. Nalbandian, by contrast, would have been much more relaxed as he strode onto Centre Court. Consequently, Nalbandian's heart rate would have been far lower than Murray's when he walked onto court and only when play started would he have started burning energy. This would have left him much more disposed to avoid cramping. Thorpe also pointed out that stopping cramping is also about learning how and when to take on fluids and minerals. In this instance, amid all the excitement and crowd pressure, Murray forgot to keep taking on fluids.

'THE PHYSICAL AGE OF A YOUNG PLAYER CAN BE VERY DIFFERENT FROM THEIR CHRONOLOGICAL AGE – BY AS MUCH AS TWO YEARS EITHER WAY.'

LTA coach Dan Thorpe on Andrew Murray's growing pains

Thorpe agreed with Petchey in saying that it was unfair to compare Murray with Nadal, saying: 'The physical age of a young player can be very different from their chronological age – by as much as two years either way. That's why it's unfair to compare Murray with Nadal, who was much more developed at 18.' He then went on to add a note of caution: 'This has to be reflected in a player's training programme. But if in another year or two he's still suffering the same problems, some serious questions have got to be asked.'

Following Wimbledon, Murray's condition came under intense scrutiny again during the US Open. He went into the Flushing Meadows tournament nursing a shoulder injury sustained in his final qualifying match against Ecuador's Giovanni Lapentti and, after emerging victorious, he raised a finger to his lips in what was clearly a symbolic message to his detractors to keep quiet. He said after the match: 'I don't think I got a lot of credit for Wimbledon about how tough it was and physically I wasn't in the best of shape. I'm young, I'm 18 years old and I don't need that at this stage in my career. Every single person in Britain is so negative about the young players. All they are waiting to do is just put them down, and I think this week I have showed that possibly I might go on and do well.'

However, further fitness questions were raised – and only partly quelled – during Murray's energy-sapping first-round match with Romania's Andrei Pavel. The sight of Murray vomiting on-court after breaking his opponent in the fifth set was both unedifying and dramatic; it illustrated Murray's ongoing physical issues and well as his unbreakable will to win. It was at once both a worrying and an inspiring sight.

Once again, on completion of what the courageous Scot rated as his best-ever win, he thrust his finger to his mouth in another gesture of defiance to the pessimists in the press. But sometimes defiance isn't enough. In the very next round, once more during a punishing, protracted match, Murray faded dramatically and crashed out of the US Open to France's Arnaud Clement.

After bravely battling back from two sets down, like a car running on empty Murray ground to a juddering halt early in the fifth set, calling for the trainer to help him combat cramp in his right thigh. It was no use, and Murray lost the set 6-0.

> **'I ran out of gas... I just lost it after I got broken. I had nothing left,'**
>
> Murray after defeat in the 2005 US Open

Murray professed to be not too disheartened by his exit, claiming: 'It's not easy coming back from two sets to love down. In the fifth set when I got broken I ran out of gas. I've been working very hard over the last nine or 10 weeks. I just lost it after I got broken. I had nothing left, but it was more mental than anything.'

But if Murray did not appear to be that bothered about the nature of his defeat plenty of other people were. Following his exit from the US Open Murray was deluged by a torrent of advice from the great and the good about how to handle his fitness issues.

The former Davis Cup captain Roger Taylor was the first to step forward, offering that attack was the best form of defence for the Scot. If he played flat-out all the time, Taylor argued, Murray's games would be long over before they got anywhere near a fourth or fifth set. Another former Davis Cup captain, Tony Pickard, agreed: 'Two sets to love up, dumping the next set makes no sense whatsoever to me.'

British tennis stalwart David Lloyd also offered his considered opinion, saying. 'If I was in charge, I would work very quickly to ascertain if the fitness problem is physical or mental. If it's physical, you can do something about it. Mental, that's something different altogether. For an 18-year-old kid to be getting tired like that on grass is a big worry. Two weeks in a row, at Queen's and Wimbledon, he got tired. The worst thing in tennis is to have a weakness, everybody else homes in on it pretty quick. It's no good playing a great five-set match and not winning it. Andrew Castle played a great five-setter against Mats Wilander once, and though he didn't win it he lived on it for about five years. Andy hasn't got that long. The next two years will decide whether or not he is going to be a world-class player.'

Matthew Syed, a former British table tennis star,

suggested that the solution to the Scot's frequent appointments with the physiotherapist was simple: relentless hard graft on the training paddock. In Syed's uncompromising view all Murray has to do was get himself to the gym and pump some iron. Of course, Syed was probably not acquainted properly with Murray's long-term and very real medical problems, but his willingness to even enter in the great debate was a good indication that everyone wanted to have their say.

Syed's analysis of Murray's problems was based on the fact that he, too, had once suffered repeatedly from cramp at a similar stage in his career. However, what worked for Syed – a rigorous fitness programme based on hours in the gym and on the running treadmill – was simply not what Murray needed.

Meanwhile, female tennis legend Martina Navratilova believed Murray's lanky physique could prove prohibitive to his progress in the future and was a key reason for his tendency to become injured. She remarked: 'I don't want to jump to conclusions but for me the biggest question mark is his health. There's no question about his talent. The question is his body. He's pretty strong but he's really long and lanky and that puts real strain on the joints.'

'IF IT ISN'T GASTRIC, IT'S CRAMP. IF IT ISN'T MUSCLE CONTRACTIONS, IT'S TENDINITIS, BUNIONS, SCIATICA, LUPUS, DEHYDRATION, RHEUMATISM, RICKETS, GOUT, PLEURISY, SCURVY OR, AS DURING A VICTORY THIS WEEK IN BANGKOK A PLAIN OLD NERVOUS HEADACHE,'

The Daily Telegraph's Matthew Norman gives a light-hearted assessment of Murray's medical problems

On a more light-hearted note, *The Daily Telegraph*'s Matthew Norman articulated the thoughts of many tennis fans when he wrote: 'Those of us with a tendency towards hypochondria will take special delight in Andy Murray reaching the world's Top 100 without ever having felt well during a set of tennis. If it isn't his back, it's his stomach. If it isn't gastric, it's cramp. If it isn't muscle contractions, it's tendinitis, bunions, sciatica, lupus, dehydration, rheumatism, rickets, gout, pleurisy, scurvy or, as during a victory this week in Bangkok a plain old nervous headache.'

Surprisingly, Murray's own mother Judy seemed to agree with Matthew Syed that what her son needed was a good workout. She was especially keen that her fellow Scot and former British Athletics coach, Frank Dick, get his hands on her boy.

Dick, a no-nonsense customer who was once

labelled 'a tough son of a bitch' by Boris Becker, had successfully coached the likes of legendary former decathlete Daley Thompson, golfer Justin Rose and Formula One racing driver Gerhard Berger. He proclaimed: 'My take on this is really very straightforward. First of all, he is 18; a young boy. So people say, "Well, other people were there at 18." But not many others have had a normal education, have had to fight to get their status in the world, travelling outside the country to get the coaching, wandering around the world trying to get the points, and knowing if they're to have a future, then they have to have a very strong technical game. How much time was there going to be to spend on an extensive fitness programme? All he had to be fit for was the world that he was in. Which, as a junior, was three-set tennis; and he won most of those in two. So he enters a world of five-set tennis and has problems... come on, you don't need a big IQ to work it out! It was a matter of priority, and the first was to build a strong technical model. To do it the other way round would not have been right.'

No roll call of experts would be complete without words of wisdom from John McEnroe: 'The good news is that many players have overcome the problem [of cramp]: the Americans Michael Chang, James Blake and Andy Roddick are three who come

A fellow fighter (and friend), Amir Khan.

immediately to mind. It's something that often affects players when they move up from three to five-set matches. I suppose it's comparable to boxers who years ago used to have to fight for 15 rounds in championship bouts instead of the usual 12. At the moment, Murray is flagging around the 13th and 14th rounds.'

And talking of boxing, which is Murray's favourite sport, Scotland's WBO Featherweight world champion Scott Harrison offered to subject his countryman to the same arduous training regime that he regularly undertakes – running up Scotland's highest mountain, Ben Nevis, carrying sand bags – in a bid to get him fighting fit.

Another pugilist, Amir Khan, went one better by inviting Murray for a sparring session at his gym in Salford in November 2005. Murray was more than happy to accept Khan's offer and declared: 'Boxers have got great upper body strength and that's one thing I'd like to work on and improve. I'd like to do some more boxing training and try and build up my strength.'

Rumours also abounded in the media that Madrid-based Spanish doctor, Angel Ruiz Cotorro, a former player and now a leading authority on sports science, was willing to come to Murray's aid. Cotorro is credited with transforming Spain's Rafael Nadal into the archetypal hulking, muscle-bound practitioner of power tennis and also oversees the training schedules of players such as Guillermo Coria and Gustavo Kuerten.

'THEY TOLD ME I WAS IN GOOD SHAPE AND THE CRAMPING WAS BECAUSE I HAD A VERY WEAK BACK. I NOW KNOW WHAT TO DO TO COMBAT IT. CRAMPING WILL NOT BE A PROBLEM IN THE FUTURE,'

Andrew Murray on his battle for fitness

However, none of the advice offered by the pundits provided Murray with the answers he needed. It was only after a two-day stay at the Institute of Sports Medicine in Paris at the end of 2005 that Murray finally discovered the solution to his persistent cramp-related problems. He explained: 'They told me I was in good shape and the cramping was because I had a very weak back. I now know what to do to combat it. Cramping will not be a problem in the future and my back will be strong and okay in Australia.'

Following his diagnosis, the Scot also dedicated himself to a stringent training regime in South Africa's Western Cape, pounding the running track to improve his speed off the mark and extending himself in the gym. Based at the idyllic Sedgefield

Andy Murray at the ringside of a fight featuring his friend Amir Khan.

coastal resort, he was also able to relax when he needed to and luxuriate in the lakes, lagoons and beautiful scenery.

Fully rested and relaxed after his South African sojourn, Murray could now consider himself in perfect shape for the rigours of another strenuous season. Always looking for positives in even the most unpromising of situations, Murray even went so far as to claim that his physical problems had only served to make him *mentally* stronger. Add to that his improving physical condition, he claimed, and he was on the way back – in better shape than ever before.

As 2006 began Murray was confident that he would never again have to raise his finger to his lips to silence his critics. From now on he would let his tennis do the talking.

CHAPTER 12

TWIN INFLUENCES

ANY TEENAGER needs a supportive shoulder to lean on from time to time, a friend or family member in whom he or she can confide. For the youthful tennis players on the senior tour this need for a confidant is enormously important. The tour can be a lonely, intimidating place, at times overwhelming and intensely pressurised, and even the most seasoned pros find it hard to cope on occasion.

Thankfully, when Andrew Murray made the quantum leap from junior to professional men's tennis in 2005 he could rely on the reassuring presence of not one but two inspirational people in his life – his mother Judy and his then coach, Mark Petchey.

These tremendous twin influences were instrumental above all others in facilitating Murray's surge up the rankings, coaxing and

Murray squares up to John McEnroe as replacement for the injured Tim Henman at the Superset event at London's Royal Albert Hall in October 2004.

cajoling their charge from the sidelines, experiencing vicariously the huge range of emotions Murray felt as he faced injury, triumph, defeat and sensational headlines, all in the space of a few short months.

So how exactly have these contrasting figures orchestrated the bittersweet symphony that was Andrew Murray's life in 2005?

Judy Murray's immeasurable input into her son's journey from provincial Scotland to the majesty of Wimbledon's Centre Court and New York's Flushing Meadows could fill a book on its own.

Of course, before she was his chief tennis cheerleader, Judy Murray was, is, Andrew's mother. The fact that his ability with a tennis racket,

Judy Murray and coach Mark Petchey encourage the teenager at Wimbledon 2005.

obvious from the earliest age, coincided with her own passion for the game forged an even stronger link between them than that enjoyed by most mothers and sons.

Yet if anyone thinks that Judy Murray is merely living out her fantasies of tennis success through her more talented son they better think again. She is simply a woman fulfilling the first duty of any mother – that of looking after her son. Witness this extract from Judy Murray's 2005 'Wimbledon Diary', as published in *The Sunday Telegraph*:

'Mum, where's my Wimbledon pass...?'

'Probably where you left it...'

'It's not...'

'Well, what were you wearing when you had it last...?'

'My tracksuit bottoms...'

'Then that's where it will be...'

'But where are my tracksuit bottoms...?'

'Right there in front of your eyes...'

'How did you expect me to see them there? You've folded them...'

Even in the maelstrom of the world event that is Wimbledon, this vignette has the universal ring of humdrum, everyday truth that any mother or son will recognise. They could just as easily have been discussing the whereabouts of Andrew's sports kit before a school sports day. The whole episode is a delightful reminder that Judy Murray and her son Andrew are essentially ordinary people whose lives are rooted in normality despite the extraordinariness of their lives in sport.

Her son may be on the cusp of tennis greatness, but Mrs. Murray is determined that, first and foremost, she will never cease to be a mum as her *The Daily Telegraph* diary perfectly illustrated:

But first of all I have a date with the hoover, duster and bin bags. Gary Richardson's coming round with a BBC film crew and Andy's been alone in the house for two hours now, which means the place will be a bomb site. Who'd be a mum? This is the start of the third week in our rented basement flat around the corner from the All England Club and, like any teenager, Andy tends to leave a trail of destruction worthy of a hurricane in his wake. Gorged on pasta, Andy returns to sprawl on the sofa in front of the DVD player to watch the Adam Sandler golf comedy *Happy Gilmore*, followed by *Ultimate Fight Boxing*. I do the ironing...

Meanwhile, her son's reaction to his mother is representative of most teenagers' – a mixture of embarrassment and appreciation. Murray knows it would be uncool to acknowledge his mother's influence too much, although he is acutely aware of how invaluable she has been to him.

Following his landmark win over Radek Stepanek at Wimbledon 2005, during which his mother was an animated and emotional onlooker in the stands, this adolescent duality was all too apparent when Murray said: 'My mum made an idiot of herself. Seriously, she has been brilliant.'

After Judy Murray was filmed crying following one of Andrew's Wimbledon victories he confessed to Sue Barker on BBC television that the sight of his mother's tears had made him cringe, as he did not want to be perceived as a 'Mummy's boy'.

The straight-talking Scot also disclosed that he was not altogether comfortable with his mother and other friends and family members watching him courtside at matches. He said: 'I don't really like anybody that I know watching except my coach. If your family and friends come to see you, you feel you have to go out for a meal with them, you have to go out to see them afterwards and you have to give them match tickets. It's quite difficult when all you want to do is concentrate on your tennis.'

Also distracting for Murray is his mother's penchant for singing in the car. He told one newspaper: 'I do want to start driving, not because I want a flash car but just because I want to get around the place. I don't want to get the tube everywhere and when you have to spend time in the car with your mum you have to listen to her singing.' Once again, the mother-son bond wins out over the teacher-pupil relationship. No matter what they achieve together in tennis, Judy and Andrew Murray will always be mother and son, first and foremost.

It is undeniable, however, that Judy Murray exceeds the expectations of a normal mother in the extraordinary lengths she has gone to in order to further her son's tennis career. The number of miles she has clocked up, ferrying her boy to tournament after tournament, at home and abroad, must be innumerable. When it comes down to it, Judy Murray will do whatever it takes to further her son's pursuit of excellence in his chosen sport.

What Judy Murray brings to the table is her own vast experience as a tennis player and coach. As a player, she won 64 Scottish titles and represented Great Britain at the World Student Games. Unlike a mother who, for example, supports her son's football or boxing interests, Judy Murray knows exactly what it is that drives her son on, what it is about tennis that he loves.

Her father, Roy Erskine, recalled: 'We had the same scenario 30 years ago with Judith. She was winning everything tennis wise – she was the Scottish champion at every age level. She was a great player and she might have achieved the same level but she got homesick. She was on the international circuit for five weeks but came home from a tournament at the age of 18, flung her bags on the floor and said "That's it, I am going to university".'

A move into the world of coaching – Murray became Scottish national coach in 1996 – was as profitable as her playing career. Her commendable efforts in implementing a training programme for talented eight to 11-year-olds in Scotland were officially recognised when she was named LTA Coach of the Year in 2003. In addition, her constant lobbying for increased funding for tennis in Scotland has won her plaudits from everyone involved in the game.

> 'She was on the international circuit for five weeks but came home from a tournament at the age of 18, flung her bags on the floor and said "That's it, I am going to university".'
>
> Roy Erskine, Andrew Murray's grandfather on Judy Murray's sudden decision to give up professional tennis

Judy Murray's coaching excellence also ensured that, by the end of 2003, three young Scottish males – her own son Andrew, Jamie Baker and David Brewer – were among the top 25 juniors in the world.

While passion, commitment and enthusiasm

have certainly contributed to her expertise, her willingness to embrace new methods and ideas also marks out Judy Murray as a coach well above the average. Her meticulous preparation for her son's matches has even involved filming his opponents and analysing the results using statistics and state-of-the-art software to pinpoint their strengths and weaknesses.

In short, Judy Murray is Andrew's mother, coach, mentor and friend. What more could a boy ask for?

The next most important person in Andrew Murray's tennis life is his coach, Mark Petchey.

In the spring of 2005, the teenager had dispensed with the services of veteran coach Pato Alvarez. Prior to the June 2005 Queen's Club tournament Murray was introduced to 34-year-old Petchey, a former British Davis Cup player who had once reached number 80 in the world.

A short-term agreement was reached whereby Petchey – then head of men's training at the Lawn Tennis Association – would oversee the Scot's fortunes during the British grass-court season. Nothing more concrete than that was agreed by either party due to Petchey's other tennis commitments.

The union had its obvious advantages; Petchey was much closer to Murray's age than Alvarez and therefore could relate more to his outlook on life.

The scurrying Scot: Murray in action during the 2005 US Open.

In the down time between matches or when on the move from tournament to tournament, Murray and Petchey were able to bond over games of backgammon or when battling it out on Murray's Playstation.

Secondly, Petchey had significant experience of representing his country during a 10-year career that was only ended by injury in 1998. He had, on several occasions, performed creditably at Wimbledon so therefore could adequately prepare the youngster for the summer.

Since giving up playing, the Englishman had created a growing reputation for himself as a coach, having steered the Croatian women Tina Pisnik and Silvija Talaja to the upper echelons of the womens' game – in Talaja's case, to a career high of 18 in the world. Petchey's down-to-earth affability and use of positive training methods were also welcome.

The cumulative effect of Petchey's influence resulted in a content, relaxed and well-prepared Murray, who responded brilliantly during the summer of 2005, leaving his coach to ponder some significant dilemmas. Was he prepared to spend weeks on end away from wife Michelle and daughters Nicole, seven, and four-year-old Myah as he embarked on what promised to be a globe-trotting adventure with his Scottish protégé? Was he also prepared to resign from one of British tennis' most prestigious roles – a coveted position that offered reassuring job security and the chance to groom a generation of potential rising stars rather than just one single – if more than promising – individual?

There was also the external issue of whether Petchey was a high-profile enough coach. Could he withstand and ignore the constant clamour for a more illustrious and more successful former tennis player to guide Dunblane's finest? Hanging over Petchey's candidature as coach was the not inconsiderable shadow of John McEnroe himself, who had already pronounced himself a Murray fan and had volunteered to train with him on a pat-time basis.

Other names were put in the frame above Petchey's, heavy hitters with the kind of take-no-prisoners attitude that the laid-back Petchey was though to be lacking. David Lloyd was one of those who had reservations about Petchey's Mr. Nice Guy character, and advised that Murray. 'Has the ability to get into the world's Top 50, and therefore to become a Top 10 player. He is as good a prospect as we have had for years. But he needs a strong person with him. He needs someone like Ion Tiriac. When Ilie Nastase was growing up, Tiriac used to grab him, physically lift him in the air, pack him off to bed. Björn Borg had Lennart Bergelin. He was brutal too. Mark Petchey is a very good guy and a pretty good coach. It is not Petch's fault, but you need a dictator type, someone exceptionally strong as a coach, like Bob Brett or Brad Gilbert.'

However, Petchey is no soft touch and has an undoubted steely side. This was in evidence when he and LTA performance director David Felgate took the decision to throw 2004 Wimbledon junior finalist Miles Kasiri off the National Tennis Training programme for three months for under-achievement. Nicknamed 'The Judge' by some young British players for his often severe pronouncements on their abilities, Petchey was not the sort of man to tolerate any waywardness from his charges.

One final charge levelled against the Essex-born coach was that he would lack credibility in giving instructions to a youngster who was destined to far

Murray's former coach, Mark Petchey, may not have achieved greatness in tennis, but you don't need to have been a great player to be a successful manager, as the likes of Chelsea supremo Jose Mourinho have proved.

exceed what he had ever achieved in tennis. This accusation was quickly batted aside with the observation that the best players rarely make the best coaches. In football terms, consider the chequered managerial career of many footballing greats who have shown they are not able to translate their wizardry into the managerial arena at the highest level. On the other hand, mediocre former players, or even non-players, such as Jose Mourinho at Chelsea and Arsène Wenger at Arsenal, were able to become superb coaches.

In the event, the doubts about Petchey were set to one side, and he himself accepted the challenge to groom and guide the country's most exciting new tennis talent.

'HE IS RECEPTIVE TO WHAT I THINK HE NEEDS FOR HIM TO GET BETTER, BUT STUBBORN AS WELL. IT'S A GREAT CHALLENGE BUT I LIKE THAT.'

Mark Petchey on coaching Andrew Murray

He outlined his reasons for taking on Murray as follows: 'I felt I did a damn good job with the two [Croatian] girls I worked with, but I understand there were those, some who had coached Grand-Slam champions, who wondered why Andy didn't want them. I always thought Andy would be good enough to get into the Top 100 and that I could help him get there and now the next stage of the journey begins. The next level is to have him challenging for major titles. I didn't walk blindly into this thinking I knew it all. My priority will always be to do what I think is best for him, as long as he wants me. I know this is going to get tougher, being away from the family for long periods. We decided I had to commit to this, they've been enormously supportive and so has Andy. He has a heart of gold as well as being as tough as nails – it's a lovely combination. He is driven and determined about making a success of his life and he's also a great person which, at 18, makes him a rare breed. He is receptive to what I think he needs for him to get better, but stubborn as well. It's a great challenge but I like that. He has an uncanny understanding of the game for one so young.'

Murray was equally thrilled to be working with Petchey. In explaining why he was so pleased to be taken on by Petchey he even forgot about his customary dislike of the LTA, admitting: 'I'm so pleased to have Mark as my coach, I respect him a great deal. The LTA have been very supportive of the plan we have put together and I appreciate their confidence and support.'

Later in the year, the grateful Scot would acknowledge Petchey's part in his breakthrough year when he received the Lawn Tennis Association Writers' Player of the Year award. 'I owe all this to Mark,' he said. 'I couldn't have done it without him. I'd also like to thank his wife for putting up with me around the house.'

This truly was a Summer of Love, and even LTA national performance director David Felgate felt moved to join in the group hug, claiming: 'To perform as Andy has under the glare of publicity shows his determination and potential. We have full confidence in Mark and believe he is the best person to guide Andy through the professional tour.'

Centre of attention: Murray makes his way through the crowds after his match against David Nalbandian at Wimbledon 2005 – a sign of his newly-acquired fame.

It was a massive shock to see Petchey and Murray part company in early 2006. Of course, there are other pivotal people in Murray's life beyond Judy Murray and Mark Petchey, each of whom can offer a range of skills and expertise.

Team Murray is an extremely professional outfit, which also includes physiotherapist Jean-Pierre Bruyere, former British rower Lisa Eyre, who provides fitness know-how, and agent Sian Masterton, who guides Murray safely through the media minefield and commercial wonderland that has opened up for him so enticingly.

Other family members, including father Will and brother Jamie, also keep him crucially grounded, as does new girlfriend Kim Sears, who provides a welcome distraction from the pressures of tennis.

Here is a youngster who is not afraid to rely on others, constantly eager to assimilate information and wisdom from those he admires, whether they are involved on tennis or not. One such Murray-approved sage is the former England rugby team coach, Sir Clive Woodward, whose advice on achieving success Murray sought out at the BBC Sports Personality Awards in 2004.

With such a strong support network, Murray appears to have everything in place that he needs to ensure ongoing and further success. The rest is up to him.

CHAPTER 13

AND THE WINNER IS…

SUCCESS, AS they say, brings its own rewards. But it also brings *awards*, and in his short career Andrew Murray has already picked up more than his fair share.

But some prizes are more important that others, especially now that award ceremonies proliferate at every turn. For British sports stars the unquestioned top of the tree is the BBC Sports Personality of the Year Award and its younger brother, the Young Sports Personality of the Year. When Andrew Murray picked up this latter gong in December 2004 it was a sure sign that he was now a major player, in every sense of the word.

Being named The Young Sports Personality of the Year was a fitting tribute to his efforts throughout a year and cemented his position as British tennis' most exciting new kid on the block. The award was especially welcome as it was voted for by the British public. Traditionally the preserve of soccer players, or athletes in an Olympic year, for the award to be picked up by a young tennis player was a massively positive sign that tennis was about to break out of its middle-class ghetto.

Murray with BBC Scotland Sports Personality of the Year award.

Murray began 2004 rated the world's second best male junior tennis player, behind Frenchman Gaël Monfils, before a long-term knee injury interrupted his quest for success for several months. However, on his return Murray picked up where he had left off by taking the US Open boys' crown, earning selection for the British Davis Cup squad and winning three Futures tournaments.

Murray' cause for inclusion in the Young Sports Personality nominations was championed on TV by children's programmes such as *Blue Peter* and *Xchange*, highlighting his youth appeal and drawing on his support among a non-adult audience. In voting for Andrew Murray, children were effectively voting for one of their own. Andrew Murray wasn't just a Man of the People, he was a man of the little people, too. Fittingly, when

Murray stepped forward to accept his award, it was presented to him by Boris Becker.

In 1985 the 17-year-old Becker took Wimbledon by storm, becoming its youngest-ever male singles winner. In handing over the Young Sports Personality award, Becker was in some sense also handing over the Presidency of what can be called the 'Young Tennis Punks' club.

And as befits an iconoclastic young punk, Murray took full advantage of the auspicious occasion by seeking out Sir Clive Woodward, introducing himself (as if it were necessary!), and buttonholing the Rugby-World-Cup-winning coach for free advice on how to cope with pressure at the highest level of sport.

A year later, the Scot's amazing exploits throughout 2005 guaranteed his graduation to the Daddy of all awards: the BBC Sports Personality of the Year. However, Murray, and other contenders such as Liverpool footballer Steven Gerrard were mere by-standers as cricketer Andrew 'Freddie' Flintoff deservedly walked away with the trophy following his pivotal role in England's nail-biting Ashes victory over Australia.

Perhaps it was all to the good that Murray lost out to Flintoff. It was a strange fact that winners of the award often suffered a slump in form in the wake of their victory. As if to reinforce the point, just hours

Sir Clive Woodward, who was approached by Andy at the 2004 BBC Sports Personality awards ceremony for some top tips.

after collecting his Sports Personality of the Year honour, Flintoff was bowled out for a duck in a one-day international in Pakistan. Of course, Flintoff's failure at the crease probably had as much to do with his staying up half the night in order to collect the award via satellite link from Pakistan than anything else, but the 'curse' of the Sports Personality of the Year still held.

Sport psychologist Rob Robson explained this phenomenon by declaring: 'Once they are voted BBC Sports Personality of the Year, they feel a tremendous pressure to perform. If they are not careful, they can begin to feel as though they have the weight of the whole nation on their shoulders.'

Back in Scotland, Murray was also earning recognition for his achievements. In 2004, he was named BBC Scotland's Young Personality and the following year picked up the senior award, fending off the challenge of golfer Colin Montgomerie, cyclist Chris Hoy, cricketer Craig Wright and boxer Scott Harrison. Murray garnered 55 per cent of the public vote and, much to his delight, received the illustrious award from Tony Mowbray, manager of his favourite football club, Hibernian.

Mowbray showered words of praise on the fêted Scot, who he invited to the Hibernian training ground. He said: 'The word that springs to mind is inspiration. The humility he seems to have should be an inspiration to the nation's young people. I hope some of it rubs off on the young players I've got in my team.'

Ensuring that the Murray mantlepiece would continue to be short of space, in 2005 he also picked up the Glasgow Lord Provost's award.

Murray received his BBC Scotland Sports Personality of the Year Award from Tony Mowbray, the manager of his favourite team, Hibernian.

Inevitably, Murray's own sport would also honour his achievements. He was crowned Young Player of the Year in 2003 and 2004. He was then voted the Lawn Tennis Association's Player of the Year in 2005, a deeply ironic accolade following Murray's savaging of the LTA earlier in the year for, in his opinion, holding back his brother's tennis career.

Given his lack of regard for the LTA's formal approach to most things, Murray turned up for the black-tie ceremony in London wearing a pair of trainers and casual clothes. But this was not so much a deliberate snub to the LTA as an expression of Murray's natural, take-it-or-leave-it personality.

That same year, Murray also scooped the Best International Newcomer award from Britain's sports writers and photographers, and in 2006 he was nominated for two honours at the ATP Stars for Stars Awards in Miami: ATP Fan Favourite and Newcomer of the Year.

Each of these awards was warmly welcomed by the engaging young Scot. But one thing is absolutely beyond doubt: he would swap them all for a Grand Slam win. For Andrew Murray, awards are secondary; it is winning matches that counts.

CHAPTER 14

HOPE FULFILLED?

AFTER AN exceptional 2005, what would 2006 hold for Andrew Murray? One thing was sure, whatever he did, whatever successess and failures he encountered, the eyes of the world would be on him. A rampant and demanding media in Britain would chart his every move, ready to heap praise upon him or pile on the agony as match results dictated. He was no longer the new kid on the block or a promising newcomer, he was Andrew Murray, the man – not boy – that a nation was pinning all of its hopes on.

The spiralling expectations surrounding Murray threatened to get out of control, so it was perhaps fitting that he would begin the new year as far away from the unremitting glare of the British media spotlight as possible – in Australia.

'THIS YEAR THE GOAL IS TO WIN THE BIG MATCHES BECAUSE IF I'M GOING TO GET INTO THE TOP 20 THEN I HAVE TO DO WELL AT THE GRAND SLAMS AND THE MASTERS SERIES TOURNAMENTS.'

Andrew Murray in January 2006

As January Down Under is the height of summer, Murray could also take comfort that he was escaping a harsh winter back home. He would take further solace from the fact that, given that this was the first time he had started a year as a senior, Murray had no ranking points to defend. He had in front of him a clear run in which to make his way up the world tennis order. He explained: 'I don't have any ranking points to defend for the first few weeks of the year, so if I do well then I think that I can reach the Top 20 by year's end. This year the goal is to win the big matches because if I'm going to get into the Top 20 then I have to do well at the Grand Slams and the Masters Series tournaments.'

He opened 2006 at the Adelaide International with what represented, on paper at least, a relatively easy start to the new campaign – a match with Italian qualifier Paolo Lorenzi. A little rusty at first, he lost the first set 3-6, but recovered to take the next two – and the match – 6-0 6-2.

Murray admitted his best form had eluded him,

Murray starts 2006 down under, determined to prove that his annus mirabilis in 2005 was not a one off.

but was nevertheless fairly pleased with the win. He said: 'The start of year it's just about getting through the first few matches, and getting your match fitness up, try and get your timing up and get used to winning again. I was happy with the way I fought but wasn't too happy with the way I played.'

However, there was to be no further chance for Murray to shake off his early season lethargy as he succumbed 7-6 4-6 6-1 to world number 24 Tomas Berdych in the next round. The teenager believed he had actually performed better than in his first-round match, but conceded that some inconsistent serving had contributed to his downfall. In any case, Murray stressed that the forthcoming Australian Open was his primary focus and insisted that he was not too perturbed at his early exit.

Next up for Murray was a trip to neighbouring New Zealand to take part in Auckland's Heineken Open, where tournament director Graham Pearce was relishing the Scot's appearance. He said: 'Each year we look to have a potential future star in the Heineken Open singles and we are pleased Andy Murray, who is clearly seen as a star on the way up, will be playing.'

Danish veteran Kenneth Carlsen opposed Murray in the first round although, as the straight-talking Scot later admitted, the blustery wind proved more difficult to contend with than his opponent. Carlsen was also troubled by an ankle injury and Murray cruised to a 7-5 6-2 victory, after which his increasing inclination towards outspokenness caused quite a stir.

Speaking to a reporter on court, he claimed that both he and Carlsen had played 'like women' in the first set, a comment that was greeted by a chorus of boos from some sections of the crowd. Murray tried to explain his mischievous comment later by saying: 'I was watching a Hopman Cup match on TV and Svetlana Kuznetsova said it after there were nine breaks in the first set, so that's why I said it.'

With the classy Croatian Mario Ancic lined up as his next opponent, Murray would have to do what a man's gotta do in the next round. Unfortunately, in a mistake-prone performance riddled with schoolboy errors, Murray went down to the big-serving Balkan 6-3 7-6.

Murray was left to regret that for the second time that year he had failed to progress when faced with a higher-ranked opponent: 'He is obviously a very good player, much more experienced than me, but I need to start winning these matches against the better players,' he said.

He was swiftly given the opportunity to do so when he was handed a match against world number 46 Juan Ignacio Chela of Argentina in the first round of the Australian Open. Victory would, in all probability, give Murray the chance to test himself against even higher-rated opposition as a mouth-watering tie against home favourite Lleyton Hewitt would be his probable second-round match.

Murray entered the tournament knowing he would have to sharpen up his serving and was also prepared to fight fire with fire if the incendiary Argentine's legendary feistiness came to the fore. The year before, Chela was fined £1,200 for allegedly spitting at Lleyton Hewitt. It was unlikely that Chela would be reckless enough to do

Murray is pumped up for his first appearance at the Australian Open in January 2006.

something that provocative again, but Murray insisted that he would be 'fired up' for anything Chela attempted against him.

'I HAD A GREAT YEAR LAST YEAR, BUT I'M STILL ONLY 18 YEARS OLD AND I'M PLAYING AGAINST GUYS WHO ARE STILL HIGHER RANKED THAN ME AND HAVE MUCH MORE EXPERIENCE. IT'S NOT THE END OF THE WORLD IF I LOSE TO THEM; IT'S JUST BETTER EXPERIENCE FOR ME.'

Andrew Murray keeps it real

He also cautioned against over-optimism. Perhaps with the pressure of shouldering a nation's hopes

Murray demonstrates his frustration at his error-strewn collapse against Chela.

finally affecting him, Murray – in uncharacter-istically talkative form – commented: 'I'm still going to go into a lot of the matches as an underdog. I think people have gone a bit over the top in expecting me to win matches against guys who are much higher ranked than me, especially when I've hardly played any ATP tournaments. So it's quite difficult for me going into the tournaments knowing that I'm expected to win a lot of the matches. I think everybody just has to keep everything in perspective. I had a great year last year, but I'm still only 18 years old and I'm playing against guys who are still higher ranked than me and have much more experience. It's not the end of the world if I lose to them; it's just better experience for me. Although I do expect a lot of myself, so I can see why people do think I'm going to do well. But everybody just has to realise it doesn't happen that easy. It's going to take a while before I play my best.'

A while indeed. With the possibility of a match against Hewitt at the back of his mind, Murray failed to concentrate on the job in hand and was demolished by Chela in straight sets: 6-1, 6-3, 6-3.

After having his serve broken in game two and again in the sixth, the under-pressure Scot committed 15 unforced errors as Chela stormed to the first set in just 23 minutes. The Argentinian cantered to the next two sets, breaking Murray twice en-route to the second round, to leave the Scot disconsolate and demoralised.

Looking for someone to blame for his below-par performance, Murray perhaps unwisely chose the post-match press conference to round on those he blamed for creating the weight of expectation around him – the media. He told the assembled press pack: 'If you guys expect me to play well every single match and every single tournament then it's not going to happen. Everybody has a bad tournament sometime. Unfortunately, it came here.'

Inevitably, the press hit back at Murray's 'moaning'. They rightly pointed out that so far he had been more than favourably portrayed in the media. Murray's response was stinging: 'You don't think there's any pressure on me?' he asked them. 'Well, if you don't think that, then I'm obviously going to disagree on something. If you guys don't think you're putting pressure on me, then that's fine. I'll forget about it.'

Murray's misery was compounded when he and the Serbian Novak Djokovic went out in the first round of the men's doubles when they lost to Fabrice Santoro and Nenad Zimonjic in straight sets, 7-6 6-3.

The fall-out from both Murray's distinctly underwhelming start to the year and his irritable reaction to it was sure to provoke a media backlash.

When the hacks are attacked they respond in kind. On the BBC Sport website, columnist Derek 'Robbo' Robson lauched a light-hearted but barbed attack on the Scot when he wrote: 'Well, I was a bit narked with Andy Murray. Everybody's had positive things to say about him and nobody really had a go at him for losing. Everyone was saying he's only 18, it's going to take time – but he got his retaliation in first by saying the media are expecting him to win every match. To be honest I think that's a bit out of order. It's perfectly legitimate for him to get thrashed by someone who's a bit better than him at the moment and there's no point in getting into a teenage strop about it.'

> **'They didn't lose that match, you did.'**
>
> Pat Cash criticises Andy Murray's attack on the press following his exit from the 2006 Australian Open

Robson then went on to twist the knife by telling the mop-topped teenager to 'get a haircut'.

Former Wimbledon champion Pat Cash, known for his uncompromisingly forthright views, also took Murray to task, commenting: 'How can he complain about the pressure put on him by the British press while accepting a bumper cheque. He has enormous potential. He could ultimately become a Top 10 player and win Grand Slam titles. However, I use the word "could" rather than "will".

The 1987 Wimbledon champion Pat Cash lashed out at the Scot for his criticism of the media at the start of 2006.

Some of the evidence I have seen brings doubt into my thinking.' Cash then went to offer some firm but fair advice: 'If he believes the press is scrutinising his every move he should stop reading newspapers and he should tell those around him he doesn't want to know what his critics are saying. It is always better to spend an extra half-hour gathering your thoughts after a tough defeat than to rush into the interview room and vent your anger on those asking questions. They didn't lose that match, you did.'

Now, more than ever, Murray needed his close-knit support network of friends and associates to rally round. One person that Murray turned to was Tim Henman, who knew a thing or two about being on the receiving end of poison pen attacks from the press. The teenage boxing sensation Amir Khan also leapt to Murray's defence, declaring: 'He's worrying too much, he just needs to chill out a bit and concentrate on his own sport. He's going through the same route as I'm going, he wants to be a champion in his sport, we're the same age and we're coping with the same media attention. You have to go in there and forget about the press and stay 100 per cent focused.'

Naturally, Mark Petchey also placed a metaphorical protective arm around his young charge. 'If we all look back to when we were 18,' he reminded the world, 'I am sure we did not make all the right decisions at the right times.' Then, in an effort to build bridges, he admitted: 'To be fair to the newspapers a lot of what they said was right on the money.' As well as being a coach, it was also Petchey's job to make sure that Murray learned how to handle himself in the full glare of the media spotlight. What Murray had to acknowledge, with Petchey's help, was that professional tennis was about much more than playing tennis. It was an intensely political sport, where a player's off-court PR was almost as important as their on-court performances. Staying on-side with the media could make a player's life a lot easier. However, Murray's youthful honesty and occasionally tetchy temper did not always make this easy. It will be interesting, to say the least, to watch how Andrew Murray's love-hate relationship with the fourth estate develops in the future.

Back on the tennis front, there were few encouraging signs for Murray that he had shrugged off the disappointment of his early exit from the Australian Open in his next tournament, in Croatia.

He took on Croatian number one Ivan Ljubicic, then ranked fifth in the world, in the first round of the Zagreb Indoors tournament. After securing the first set 6-4 Murray, struggling in an intimidating arena filled with passionate fans cheering on local boy Ljubicic, surrendered the final two sets, 6-2 6-3.

If the start to Murray's year had been dismal, downbeat, fractious and under-whelming, the next phase of the season would be its absolute antithesis: delightful, jubilant and hugely inspiring. Murray's growing army of fans were about to be served with a stupendous and remarkable reminder of the fickleness of sport.

'IT'S MUCH MORE RELAXED HERE. IT'S A LITTLE EASIER TO CONCENTRATE ON TENNIS. THE QUESTIONS ARE A BIT EASIER – THEY'RE ONLY USUALLY ABOUT TENNIS. AT HOME, EVEN THE SMALLEST THING YOU SAY IS PICKED UP ON.'

Andrew Murray on America

It is perhaps unsurprising that Murray's impending reversal of fortune would be kick-started by a trip to America, a country in whose go-for-it atmosphere he thrives. It was with high hopes that Murray left Eastern Europe and headed for the US, to take part in San Jose's SAP Open. As soon as Murray arrived he felt more comfortable, declaring: 'It's much more relaxed here. It's a little easier to concentrate on tennis. The questions are a bit easier – they're only usually about tennis. At home, even the smallest thing you say is picked up on.'

The Scot looked like a player reborn as he took to the court for his match against America's Mardy Fish. Bubbling with energy and displaying a ruthless efficiency that had been missing from his game so far that year, Murray disposed of his first-round opponent 6-2 6-2.

Firing down five aces, losing his serve only once and converting six of his 11 break-point chances, Murray put in an enormously productive day at the office. The revitalised Scot afterwards attributed his dramatic improvement in form to constant serving practice, commenting: 'That's the best match I've played this year so far. I feel like I'm hitting well and I was moving well. I've been struggling with my serve but I've practised a lot in the last couple of weeks and I was happy with my serve tonight.'

Also a source of delight for Murray was the fact that he had avenged a three-set defeat to Fish in Indianapolis in the summer of 2005. He admitted: 'Since I played him last year, this time I knew his strengths and weaknesses and it helped me get my position early in the rally. I was aggressive on the right balls and I was taking risks and I played a really solid match. I'm really happy with how it went.'

Next up was unheralded Taiwanese prospect Yeu-Tzuoo Wang, who had caused an upset by knocking out America's James Blake in the opening round. As a relatively unknown quantity, the Taiwanese player

Andy Murray regards Tim Henman as a great source of inspiration and advice.

represented a potentially tricky obstacle for Murray. Consequently, one or two eyebrows were raised when Murray fell 3-0 behind in the first set. However, once he had the measure of his opponent Murray quickly moved through the gears to secure a relatively straightforward 6-4 6-2 win.

This meant that Murray had now progressed to his first ATP tour quarter-final of the season, and only the third of his career. Standing in his way of a semi-final spot was Sweden's Robin Soderling.

Once again slow out of the blocks, Murray dropped the first set 4-6, afterwards admitting that the late finish of his previous game had left him feeling sluggish. But, displaying the battling qualities on which his reputation had been founded, Murray fought back to take the next two sets 7-5 6-4, sealing a hard-fought victory. It had been a bumpy ride, however, as Murray took out his frustrations first on his racket – which he hurled about the court no fewer than four times – and then on the umpire, Norm Chryst, who consequently issued a code violation to the passionate Celt for swearing.

'YOU DON'T WANT TO BE UNPOPULAR ON TOUR, BUT WHEN YOU ARE ON THE COURT YOU HAVE TO DO WHAT YOU HAVE TO DO TO WIN.'

Andrew Murray develops a winning mentality

The Scot's outburst, which caused Soderling to complain to the umpire, was waved away by Murray afterwards: 'I was trying to get myself going because I started the match so sloppy. It obviously worked. I was a little frustrated at the four or five bad calls on big points. You don't want to be unpopular on tour, but when you are on the court you have to do what you have to do to win.'

Be careful what you wish for Andrew: if it was

unpopularity that he was courting, he was handed the opportunity in the semi-final, when he came up against home favourite Andy Roddick. Nick-named A-Rod because of his missile-like serve, Roddick, backed by a partisan crowd, was bound to be a tough opponent.

A former US Open champion and world number three, Roddick was chasing his third consecutive win in the San Jose tournament and was as keyed up for the game as Murray. It promised to be a match that would be decided on the tightest of margins, either on a few unforced errors or some inspired, well-timed returns of serve. And it was Murray whose game came together at the right time to seal a sensational 7-5 7-5 victory.

Murray was almost overcome with emotion after surging through to his second ATP tour final in what was his first-ever win against a Top 10 opponent. He said: 'I have so much respect for a guy like Roddick. He's achieved so much. It's great just to be on the court with him. To beat him is amazing. I was almost a little sick because of nerves but in the end I came though. Beating Roddick in his home country is like a dream come true.' Surprisingly, the usually affable Roddick was only at best grudging in his praise for Murray after the match, preferring to berate himself instead for failing to crank up his famed big serve.

After an indifferent start to 2006, Murray achieves remarkable redemption at the SAP Open in San Jose in February where he accounts for Mardy Fish, Yeu-Tzuoo Wang, Robin Soderling and Andy Roddick en-route to the final.

Murray's opponent in the final was Lleyton Hewitt, a player who in many ways served as the template for Murray: passionate, rugged and at times uncouth. The game promised to be a thrilling clash, and that is exactly what it turned out to be.

First off, Murray had a small psychological obstacle to overcome. A quick glance at the form book revealed that Hewitt had won all eight of his previous encounters with players outside the Top 50 in major finals. Thankfully, Andrew Murray is not the type of person to give too much thought to the facts and figures of tennis. In his eyes, you play tennis with a racket not with a form book.

In addition, Murray felt that he had a point to prove. Hewitt was exactly the type of player he had to beat if he wanted to be mentioned in the same breath as him as a top player.

Yet once the match got under way the gritty Australian looked on course for a routine victory. He broke Murray three times in an accomplished first set to take a 6-2 lead. However, Murray dug deep and played some fantastic tennis to win the next set 6-1. The courageous Scot started the third set with the same vigour and purpose, surging to a 2-0 lead before a poor line call halted his momentum and allowed Hewitt a way back into the match. Undeterred, Murray redoubled his efforts to claw his way to a 4-2 advantage. Then it was Hewitt's turn to display some heroics, taking the next two games to level matters at 4-4.

The match was turning into a classic, with both players giving their all in front of an engrossed crowd. Inevitably, the final set was taken to a nerve-shredding tie break, the tennis equivalent of a penalty shoot-out. Murray took a 3-0 lead but Hewitt revived to close the deficit to 5-3, at which point the serve reverted to the Scot. Showing an admirable absence of nerves, Murray closed out the match with two bludgeoning serves.

Murray declared that his maiden ATP tour victory was 'a dream come true' and that his thrilling San Jose exploits represented, 'the best week of my life'. Sounding like the excitable teenager that he was at heart, Murray added:

I thought I played really well and got my tactics right, but didn't execute them well in the first set. Lleyton came up with some really big serves when I had my first two match points and I almost let him back in, but I managed to come through. I got a little too nervous but I managed to come through. I woke up at 3:00 a.m. and couldn't sleep because it was hard to come to terms with the fact that I'd beaten a former number one in the world in Roddick, but then I woke up this morning feeling pretty good. I controlled my emotions well out there and it feels pretty good right now. I made too many mistakes in the first set, but once I got my first break I started playing more aggressively and with more confidence. My confidence is going to be a bit higher now as well. Those are the first two guys I've beaten in the Top 10 and I'm really looking forward to the next few weeks.

'IT IS THE FIRST TIME SHE HAS COME TO A TOURNAMENT WITH ME, AND MAYBE I HAVE BEEN A LITTLE MORE RELAXED ON COURT! I PLAYED REALLY WELL AND HOPEFULLY SHE WILL COME TO A FEW MORE TOURNAMENTS.'

Andrew Murray pays tribute to Kim Sears after his first
ATP Tour victory

Perhaps a little over-excited by his triumph, Murray marked his victory in a manner reminiscent of Pat Cash's celebration of his 1987 Wimbledon victory. Climbing into the crowd, he sought out his girlfriend, Kim Sears, and indulged in a very public display of affection with the slightly-startled young lady. Once he had disengaged his lips from Sears's, Murray was able to declare: 'It is the first time she has come to a tournament with me, and maybe I have been a little more relaxed on court! I played really well and hopefully she will come to a few more tournaments.'

Hewitt, meanwhile, was magnanimous in defeat, paying generous tribute to the victor. 'I guess there haven't been too many 18-year-olds in the last five years or so with that kind of skill,' he said. 'He hits the ball extremely well, he mixes it up extremely well. He can dictate when he wants to, but he is also very good on the defence. I think he's a guy

253

Andy defeats Australia's Lleyton Hewitt in the final of the ATP tournament in 2006.

who's confident out there and that's what it takes to make it on the tour at a young age.'

A place in the Top 50, a cheque for £50,000 and the restoration of his position as Britain's media darling were among the rich rewards for Murray following his awe-inspiring conquest of Hewitt.

A further dividend was that Murray shortly afterwards replaced Tim Henman as the British number one.

'THE SKY IS THE LIMIT, IT REALLY IS. A LOT OF TIME THERE IS HYPE AND PEOPLE TALKING ABOUT PLAYERS WHEN DEEP DOWN THEY KNOW IT'S NOT GOING TO HAPPEN, BUT THIS TIME YOU HAVE A GUY THAT IS REALLY CAPABLE OF BEING A GREAT PLAYER.'

John McEnroe on Andrew Murray becoming the
British number one

John McEnroe, was one of the first to acclaim the newly-crowned King Murray of Scotland, declaring: 'I predicted a few months ago that Murray would be in the Top 20 around Wimbledon and I think there is an excellent chance of that happening. You see a guy like Murray and you see the potential that is there. The sky is the limit, it really is. A lot of time there is hype and people talking about players when deep down they know it's not going to happen, but this time you have a guy that is really capable of being a great player. He has a way of keeping you off balance, he has a feel for the game and he's playing with the most confidence he has ever had. The issue with him is probably more physical than mental. Mentally he's proven to be a pretty tough customer and his body has grown as well recently. He doesn't seem to need a whole lot of help. Mark Petchey is doing a great job but Andy believes in himself and his attitude is something that I like. He plays hard, he shows a lot of emotion.'

As a sure sign that Murray was the real deal, the bookmakers immediately slashed the odds on Murray's chances of success in all tournaments for 2006. William Hill knocked him down to 16/1 from 25/1 to win Wimbledon and also quoted him at 10/1 to win any Grand Slam event during the year.

He was rated 3/1 to beat world number one Roger Federer during the year and at 1/2 to win at least another ATP event in 2006. He was also installed as the 8/1 early favourite to become the BBC Sports Personality of the Year. Naturally, at 2/5 he was the hot favourite to end the year as British number one.

A frenzied media was also keen to groom Murray and his new partner Kim, the daughter of ex-LTA coach Nigel Sears, as Britain's new celebrity couple. However, Kim quickly dismissed suggestions that she and her Scottish suitor were about to become the next Posh and Becks.

Thankfully for Murray, not long after his media-hogging feats he was able to resume action on a tennis court, the environment in which he feels most comfortable.

His three-set victory over South Africa's Rik de Voest at the Morgan Keegan Championships in Memphis, accompanied by Tim Henman's early exit from the ABN AMRO tournament in Rotterdam, saw Murray officially replace the Englishman as Britain's number one in late February 2006.

'IT'S NOT REALLY THAT BIG A DEAL. OBVIOUSLY YOU'D RATHER BE BRITISH NUMBER ONE THAN BRITISH NUMBER 20. I'D MUCH RATHER HAVE A HIGHER WORLD RANKING THAN BRITISH, BECAUSE YOU DON'T PLAY ANY TOURNAMENTS THAT ARE JUST BRITISH PLAYERS.'

Andrew Murray 'celebrates' becoming the country's top tennis player in February 2006

As is his wont, Murray played down this latest honour: 'It's not really that big a deal. Obviously you'd rather be British number one than British No.

20. I'd much rather have a higher world ranking than British, because you don't play any tournaments that are just British players. You're competing against the whole world – and that's where you get your credit from the players from. If you're No. 1 in your country it's obviously nice, but it doesn't mean anything to the other players – whereas if you're in the Top 10 in the world that's pretty special.'

Germany's Rainer Schuttler was the next victim of the fantastic Scot, who overcame his opponent 1-6, 7-5, 6-2. Murray attributed his gritty win to his new-found confidence at having beaten the likes of Roddick and Hewitt in recent weeks. An exhausting few weeks finally took their toll when Robin Soderling ended the Scot's run of seven successive victories in the quarter-final of the Tennessee tournament, the Swede running out an easy 6-1, 6-4 winner.

His loss was a salutary reminder to the teenager that he would have to increase his physical fitness to stand any chance of Grand Slam success in the future. But what Andrew Murray has done is given himself a platform from which to launch himself to ever-greater heights.

EPILOGUE

IF 2005 had been eventful for Andrew Murray, then 2006 was promising to be even more full of incident and intrigue.

There was an alluring unpredictability to this young Scot whose fluctuating fortunes at the start of his second year as a professional made for compelling viewing, confirming him as a compelling tennis personality.

After securing his maiden ATP Tour title, Murray was widely expected to surge upwards to even giddier heights and capture more trophies along the way. But let's not forget Murray is a mercurial Brit, meaning he is prone to the odd lapse or two. Indeed, as with any teenager growing up, there are times when not everything runs smoothly.

This was certainly the case from March onwards when the teenager's career would, momentarily at least, plummet downwards as he made a series of miserable early exits from tournaments. An ankle ligament injury and bacterial infection added to the Scot's escalating woes, and also contributed to the recurrence of the dreaded cramp during his 6-4 6-7 5-7 defeat against Frenchman Jean-Rene Lisnard in the first round of the Monte Carlo Masters.

His injuries also spoilt his next Davis Cup outing when he was ruled out of the opening singles matches for Britain against Serbia and Montenegro in April 2006. Even worse for the ailing teenager, the tie had been hyped up as a triumphant homecoming for the Scot as it was staged at the Braehead Arena in Glasgow – the first time that Great Britain had played a Davis Cup match in Scotland since 1970 when they took on Austria in Edinburgh.

With the scores level at 1-1 after the opening day, the scene was set for Murray and partner Greg Rusdeski to storm to victory against Nenad Zimonjic and Ilia Bozoljac in front of a passionate Scottish crowd. However, Murray's story does not always resemble comic books and fairy tales, and a dispiriting 3-6 6-3 3-6 4-6 loss instead of the anticipated heroic victory ensued.

Not only did the disgruntled Scot look distinctly out of sorts after his injury-lay off, but his temper got the better of him when he launched a verbal volley at umpire Adel Aref.

'We got an absolutely shocking call in the first game of the fourth set, and I told the umpire how bad he was,' Murray admitted afterwards with customary, no-holds-barred honesty. He and his team-mates were fined £1,434 for his indiscretion, although this was an insignificant penalty in the context of both a lacklustre doubles defeat and overall 3-2 loss to Serbia and Montenegro.

As a collective unit, Britain's prospects of Davis Cup success were now bleak as they looked forward to an Euro-Africa Zone relegation play-off against Israel in July 2006. Greg Rusedski was a fading force and the likes of Arvind Parmar and Alex Bogdanovic had yet to prove their pedigree in the white-hot atmosphere of Davis Cup competition. At least Britain could, injury permitting, call on one Andrew Murray.

However, Murray himself chose to no longer call on his coach Mark Petchey in early April when he sprang a spring shock and surprisingly parted company with the Englishman. Murray declared that he had made his momentous and entirely unexpected decision due to a difference in opinion over his tennis career. Once again, he was displaying the tough streak which had characterised his dismissal of previous coach, Pato Alvarez, the year before.

A philosophical Petchey said of being relieved of

his duties: 'I am very proud of what we have achieved together – getting Andy into the top 50 and winning his first ATP title at the age of 18. I have no doubt that Andy will make the top 10 and be a Grand Slam winner in the future and I wish him every success.'

Meanwhile, an assured Andy said he would take his time finding a successor to Petchey, displaying yet more evidence that he possessed a steely single-mindedness and self-belief belying his tender years, as well as a growing maturity.

He remarked: 'With some important events coming up, I don't want to make a mistake and bring someone in quickly and have problems. I'm going to take my time, see who's available and make the right decision. It's about finding the right person for my tennis, and I'm confident I will make the right decision.'

For a tennis prodigy who has had no less a figure than John McEnroe drooling and clamouring to become his coach, it was clear Murray would not be short of offers from a gaggle of high-profile gurus. First to thrust his hand in the air from the scramble of wannabe suitors was Nick Bollettieri, the legendary 74-year-old American coach who guided the likes of Andre Agassi, Monica Seles and Maria Sharapova to greatness. He contacted Murray's team to express his interest in helping the youngster mature, although discounted becoming involved with him on a day-to-day basis.

Bollettieri advanced his claims for the coveted coaching role to the BBC as follows: 'I have something to offer as part of a team. There can be a role for an older guiding hand to offer advice, perspective, sometimes one-on-one intensive sessions ahead of big events. It's the job I think I could do for Andy.' The veteran American then employed some good, old-fashioned flattery to try to win over Murray, adding: 'Why do I want to work with Andy Murray? He has natural talent, that's a given, and attitude in spades. I've likened him before to Jim Courier, the ultimate workhorse, because I see his determination to give his all, and he's got that radical streak I saw in a young Agassi when I was his coach. He knows his mind and is not afraid to voice it.'

Murray's potential was certainly there for all to see and the chances were he would hook up with an experienced mentor to help him realise his youthful promise rather than continue going it alone for too long. So, within a matter of months of 2006, Andrew Murray's action-packed adventure of a career had already featured controversy, success, failure and injury – not to mention a few surprises along the way.

Expect more of the same as the wonderboy becomes a man.

ANDREW MURRAY FACTFILE

FACT FILE

Full name: Andrew Barron Murray
Date of birth: 15 May 1987
Place of birth: Dunblane, Scotland
Nationality: British
Height: 1m 88cm (6ft 2in)
Weight: 68kg (150lb)
Tennis grip: right-handed (double-handed backhand)
Turned professional: 2005
Favourite surface(s): Clay/hard courts
Parents: Mum, Judy; Dad, Will
Siblings: One brother, Jamie
Hobbies: Boxing, golf, football, go-kart racing,
Playstation, cinema, music
Favourite film: *The Girl Next Door*
Favourite music: Coldplay, Eminem, Black Eyed Peas
Clothes sponsor: Fred Perry
Racket sponsor: Head

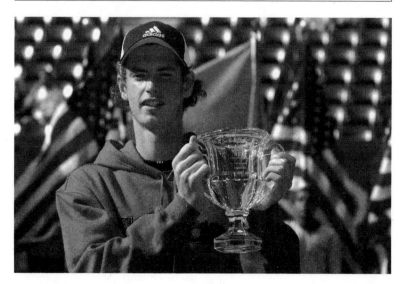

MURRAY'S MILESTONES

TOURNAMENT SUCCESSES AND AWARDS

ATP tour titles

19/2/06 beats Lleyton Hewitt in SAP Open in San Jose, USA, 2-6 6-1 7-6.

Exhibition titles

Aberdeen Cup 2005, helps Scotland beat England by 4.5 points to 2.5 points in November 2005.

Challenger titles

Beats Rajeev Ram 6-4 6-3 in Aptos, California (11/07/05)

Beats Alejandro Falla 7-6 6-3 in Binghampton, New York (8/8/05)

Futures titles

Beats Toni Baldellou 6-2 6-4 in the Spain F17, Xativa (2/8/04)

Beats Dominique Coene 6-0 6-3 in Italy F22, Rome (23/8/04)

Beats Andis Juska 1-6 6-3 7-5 in Spain F34, Orense (6/12/04)

Beats Nicolas Tourte 6-4 5-7 7-5 in Spain F34A, Pontevedra (13/12/04)

Beats Steve Darcis 6-3 3-6 6-3 in Great Britain F10, Glasgow (22/9/03)

Junior Grand Slam titles
Beats Sergiy Stakhovsky 6-4 6-2 in US Open Junior Tennis Championships, Flushing Meadows, New York (12/09/04)

Major awards
Best International Newcomer 2005 (voted by Britain's sports writers and photographers)
BBC Young Sports Personality of the Year 2004
BBC Scotland Sports Personality of the Year 2005
BBC Scotland Young Sports Personality of the Year 2004
Lawn Tennis Association Player of the Year 2005, and Young Player of the Year 2004 and 2003.

MURRAY'S TOP 10 MEMORABLE MATCHES

19 February, 2006, against Lleyton Hewitt (AUS) in SAP Open final in San Jose, USA

Murray beats former world number one Hewitt in sensational style, 2-6 6-1 7-6, to capture his first ATP tour title. After slipping behind, he shows admirable guts and determination to roar back into contention before surviving a great test of nerve in the third set tiebreak, which he edges 7-5. Almost as memorable as his performance is the sight of Murray bursting into the crowd to find his girlfriend Kim Sears – who he clumsily tries to kiss!

18 February, 2006, against Andy Roddick (USA) in SAP Open semi-final in San Jose, USA

Murray confounds all expectations by overcoming top seed and three-time former champion Roddick in a gripping, close-fought battle 7-5 7-5. Murray broke the world number three's much-vaunted serve three times on the way to a shock victory.

25 October, 2005, against Tim Henman (GBR) in first round of Davidoff Swiss Indoors in Basel, Switzerland.

A power shift, a changing of the guard, a handover of the baton – call it what you want, Murray stunningly signalled that he was the coming man in British tennis by beating the player who has been a mainstay for his country for the last 10 years. It was not a classic, but Murray more than deserved his 6-2 5-7 7-6 success which rendered him speechless and on the verge of tears.

1 October, 2005, against Paradorn Srichaphan (THA) in semi-final of the Thailand Open in Bangkok

Never mind the fact that Srichaphan suffered from cramp in the final set, to beat the Thai in front of his adoring fans was a monumental achievement for the young Scot. He reached his first ATP tour final by winning 6-7 7-5 6-2.

23 June, 2005, against Radek Stepanek (CZE) in second round of Wimbledon

This was the match that confirmed Murray's arrival on the tennis scene as a performer of some note. Stepanek is one of the most awkward opponents on the men's tour, but he was completely outplayed and outfoxed by the classy Scot, who delighted a partisan Court One crowd by earning a resounding 6-4 6-4 6-4 triumph.

21 June, 2005, against George Bastl (SUI) in first round of Wimbledon

What a dream Wimbledon senior debut this was for Murray, who would have been forgiven for being wracked by tension and nerves, especially considering that he had been an injury doubt for his home tournament. He belied his tender years with a magnificent display, outwitting his Swiss opponent with an array of brilliant ground strokes to record a routine 6-4 6-2 6-2 win on Court Two.

5 March, 2005, with David Sherwood in Davis Cup doubles for Great Britain versus Israel in Europe/Africa Zone I tie in Tel Aviv, Israel

Murray makes a stunning Davis Cup debut with Sherwood in a marvellous 6-4 7-6 2-6 7-6 win over Jonathan Erlich and Andy Ram, the number-eight-ranked doubles partnership in the world. The Scot is an inspirational figure throughout, both in his play and encouragement to himself and to his partner, as Britain take a 2-1 lead in the contest which eventually becomes a 3-2 tie win over their Israeli counterparts.

30 August, 2005, against Andrei Pavel (ROM) in first round of US Open at Flushing Meadows, New York

Murray shows his enormous strength of character by overcoming both searing heat and a bout of on-court sickness – brought on by a sodium-rich drink – to prevail in a titanic tussle 6-3 3-6 3-6 6-1 6-4. Afterwards, he hails the hard-fought triumph as his best win to date and expresses the hope that suspicions about his ability to withstand protracted matches are consigned to the history books. Sadly, he exits the US Open in the next round in another gruelling five-setter, succumbing to France's Arnaud Clement.

30 September, 2005, against Robby Ginepri (USA) in quarter-final of the Thailand Open in Bangkok

Ginepri reached the semi-final at the US Open earlier that month, but couldn't progress to the last four here as Murray shows his penchant for beating higher-ranked players by storming to a 4-6 6-4 6-3 win. It guarantees Murray his first ATP tour semi-final.

27 November, 2005, against Greg Rusedski in Aberdeen Cup for Scotland versus England clash in Aberdeen, Scotland.

The proud Scot returns to his roots and rewards a frenzied Scottish crowd with a 4-6 6-4 6-1 over his British rival to power Scotland to a 4.5-2.5 victory over the Auld Enemy in the inaugural Aberdeen Cup. Although Rusedski was hampered by a calf injury, Murray showed his ruthless streak to take full advantage, avenging his 5-7 6-7 defeat to the Canadian-born Brit the previous day.

MURRAY'S MISCELLANY

He wears size 12 shoes – the largest size provided by his sponsor, Adidas, for any of its players.

He prides himself on being able to reel off verbatim sketches from the smash-hit BBC comedy series, *The Office*.

Bagels are his favourite food for breakfast.

His sporting hero is Muhammad Ali and boxing is his favourite sport. His current favourite boxers are Ricky 'The Hitman' Hatton and Joe Calzaghe.

A massive music fan, his favourite CD is *Encore* by American rapper Eminem, although he also appreciates the more mellow sounds of British indie favourites, Coldplay.

Murray was born in 1987, the Chinese year of the rabbit, the luckiest of all the signs.

He says he welcomes female attention, and has even started receiving lacy underwear in his fan mail. However, he insists he will not marry for years.

He shares the same name as a 19th century Scottish botanist, a successful Canadian ice hockey coach and an Australian politician.

His name originates from 12th-century Scotland, in the then Pictish province Moray, in the area surrounding Inverness, which was under the rule of King David I.

His favourite film is the comedy *The Girl Next Door.*

He used wear a pair of denim shorts with pink cycling shorts underneath in homage to his hero, Andre Agassi.

Although not an inveterate reader, he cites his favourite book as being *Harry Potter and the Prisoner of Azkaban.*

Between matches, Murray likes nothing better than playing 'Pro Evolution Soccer' and 'Fight Night 2' on his Playstation.

He believes players should be allowed to listen to music courtside between games.

Robinson's Barley water and Sprite are his favourite drinks.